BEGINNING
BODYBUILDING

BEGINNING BODYBUILDING

REAL MUSCLE/REAL FAST

JOHN LITTLE
Author of MAX CONTRACTION TRAINING

New York   Chicago   San Francisco   Lisbon   London   Madrid   Mexico City
Milan   New Delhi   San Juan   Seoul   Singapore   Sydney   Toronto

The McGraw·Hill Companies

4 5 6 7 8 9 10 11 12 13 14 15 16 17 18   CCW/CCW   1 9 8 7 6 5 4 3 2 1

ISBN 978-0-07-149576-9
MHID   0-07-149576-2

Library of Congress Cataloging-in-Publication Data

Little, John R., 1960–
    Beginning bodybuilding : real muscle/real fast / John Little.
        p.   cm.
    Includes index.
    ISBN 0-07-149576-2
    1. Bodybuilding.   I. Title.

    GV546.5.L539   2008
       613.7'13—dc22   2007041982

Cover design by Tom Lau
All photos courtesy of Jason Mathas

McGraw-Hill books are available at special quantity discounts to use as premiums and sales promotions or for use in corporate training programs. To contact a representative, please e-mail us at bulksales@mcgraw-hill.com.

This book is dedicated to my wife, Terri, and to our children, Riley, Taylor, Brandon, and Benjamin, who provide inspiration and motivation in ways that championship physiques cannot even approximate, and who have added so much love, humor, and enjoyment (and drama) to their parents' lives.

Contents

Acknowledgments

The author wishes to thank several people who, directly and indirectly, contributed to the publication of this book. Jason Mathas deserves particular mention for the exceptional photography that graces the pages of this book. Jason has spent many years photographing the top physiques in the world and knows how to capture the perfect image that both inspires and educates the viewer.

Chris Lund gave me my start in bodybuilding writing and encouraged me to continue to do research into the cause-and-effect nature of muscle growth. He liked the content and saw fit to publish it in Great Britain throughout the 1980s. This resulted in my developing a following and allowed me to continue to do more research and to refine what I had learned.

Mike Mentzer was a close friend and an individual who taught me much about productive bodybuilding exercise. Although he passed away in 2001, the principles he espoused and perfected have remained my touchstones in bodybuilding science. Mike was also the first bodybuilder to actively encourage independent thought and embrace the scientific method, which has resulted in more bodybuilders training harder, training for shorter periods, and training far less frequently.

Introduction

Bodybuilding is one of the healthiest activities anybody can engage in.

Bodybuilding is probably the healthiest activity that any individual can perform. The scientific literature documents that resistance exercise not only serves to induce positive physiological changes but also can help to enhance and maintain our functional ability in later life. While this is all to the good, it remains true that the first reason most people have for working out is to improve their appearance, and in this respect, bodybuilding is without peer in the fitness world.

Running, for example, being an activity that is restricted predominantly to the lower body, cannot significantly improve your upper-body strength, nor can it enhance your flexibility. Stretching or yoga can enhance your flexibility, within certain genetically determined limits, but neither can improve your cardiovascular efficiency to any meaningful degree.

Proper bodybuilding exercise will make you stronger, enhance your flexibility, and improve your cardiovascular conditioning—in addition to dramatically altering your lean body mass (muscle) composition. As a result, your metabolic rate will rise significantly, which can lead to reduced bodyfat levels, lower blood pressure, lower cholesterol levels, and an improved sense of well-being. All of this adds up to better health and fitness and a more positive self-image. Not a bad return for an activity that requires only minutes a week of your time and that you can continue for the rest of your life.

Some of my readers may wonder why, as one who has been a staunch advocate of three ultra-intense methods of bodybuilding training (Power Factor Training, Static Contraction Training, and Max Contraction Training), I am offering in this book a more conventional protocol. The answer is simple: As not everyone has access to either vintage Nautilus machines, which are getting scarcer by the year, or Max Contraction equipment (maxcontraction.com), I felt there was a legitimate need for a valid training guide, based on well-settled principles of exercise science, that incorporates more conventional forms of equipment. Since virtually every home gym and all commercial gyms have free weights and some exercise machines, and since these pieces of equipment (mainly due to cost) are not going away anytime soon, it makes sense that most people will use this type of equipment in their workouts. However, it does not follow that most people know how to use this equipment, or that they know how to do so in a manner that will produce the results they so earnestly seek. This book will correct this deficiency and put the newcomer on the path to bodybuilding success.

Additionally, some of my readers will wonder why I'm advocating within these pages a slightly greater frequency of training (two to three times a week, as opposed to once a week) than I have recommended in my other books. It is a good question, and the answer is that from a biological standpoint, the newcomer to bodybuilding is not yet strong enough to make the kind of demands on the body's recovery ability that would necessitate a more intense and less frequent training protocol. As the beginner grows stronger, however, the training frequency will have to be reduced to once a week, and perhaps even once every two weeks. For the beginning bodybuilder, though, that time is not yet at hand.

After having worked out now for a span of more than thirty years, and with all manner of methods and equipment, I have learned what exercises work and what ones do not, as well as which machines are effective and which are not. In addition, I've learned a great deal about the biology of bodybuilding that seems to have eluded most other fitness and bodybuilding authors, particularly in regard to its effect on human recovery ability and workout volume. A disturbing trend within our industry is to look to our champions to guide us, apparently oblivious to the superior genetic disposition these champions

Advanced trainees should emphasize the position of full muscular contraction and reduce both the volume and frequency of their workouts.

possess. Also, while the industry is loath to admit it, the insidious increase in the use of steroids and other growth drugs has distorted bodybuilding, creating grotesque freaks in place of the finely built human bodies we observed when drugs were not as proliferative and bodybuilders (such as John Grimek and Steve Reeves) actually lived to a ripe old age.

Beginning Bodybuilding is concerned with your getting to your bodybuilding destination—a bigger, more muscular body—without jeopardizing your health. Within the pages of this book I have laid out facts for the beginning bodybuilder that will serve as a road map to navigate him or her away from blind alleys, dead ends, and other detours from the ultimate goal of a healthier, more muscular body.

The material in this book is intended for the absolute beginner to bodybuilding and will safely guide him or her to the intermediate and early advanced stages of development. For those seeking the "next step" in training, I recommend my books *Max Contraction Training* (McGraw-Hill, 2003) and, particularly, *Advanced Max Contraction Training* (McGraw-Hill, 2006), which go into far greater detail about the obstacles and barriers that need to be surmounted in order to make continued progress at this level of development.

For the beginning bodybuilder, the book you are holding represents the perfect guide to starting down the immensely enjoyable and personally empowering path to a stronger, healthier you. It is my hope that you enjoy the journey as much as the destination.

PART 1

Beginning Your Bodybuilding Journey

Getting Started

If you are thinking about starting bodybuilding and would like to pack on up to thirty pounds of muscle mass, then you're on the right page of the right book. The chapters that follow will provide you with all of the latest training and nutritional information needed to make it to the top of the sport, should you choose to climb that high, or—closer to ground level—just improve to the point of being the best-built person on your street.

How far you want to go in bodybuilding is ultimately a matter of your desire and disposition. Regardless, at no time are the gains any quicker or more enjoyable than during the first six months of starting a training program. It is at this juncture that bodybuilders, whether young or old, first become truly aware of their bodies and notice profound changes starting to happen. As the bodybuilder becomes more experienced, that detection is less novel, but I suppose that, on the whole, it's just as enjoyable.

KNOWING WHERE YOU STAND PHYSICALLY

It's of paramount importance when starting a bodybuilding program that you know your existing physical condition. In fact, an annual physical examination is recommended for all people, whether they engage in bodybuilding or not. If your physician gives you the OK to initiate your program (and that's likely to happen, unless you're on your last legs, in which case you'd be better off tending to your estate than adding an inch to your arms), then—and only then—you can proceed.

The program on which you're about to embark will, if followed to the letter, improve your health, strength, and muscle mass to such a degree that you and those who know you will be shocked at the metamorphosis. If you're drastically underweight, it is quite possible for you to gain up to thirty pounds of rock-hard muscle mass. If you're overweight with no discernible muscle shape, be prepared to become firm, develop a V taper, lose inches off your waist, and mold and expand your chest, shoulders, legs, and arms! Anyway, enough talking about it. Let's start making it happen!

THE JARGON OF BODYBUILDING

Bodybuilders are a genuine subculture of the population. Consequently, they often use an idiom that, to outsiders, can sound as foreign as Caesar's Latin. Terms such as *reps*, *bi's*, *tri's*, *supersets*, *preexhaustion*, *forced reps*, and *negatives* are common usage among devotees, but they can leave the initiate looking for the nearest encyclopedia! Fortunately, the specialized vocabulary is not as intimidating as it may appear, and it's not even necessary for the beginner to learn more than a quarter of it, since many terms in the jargon relate to more advanced techniques, those designed to add muscle mass to the seasoned physique. We will concentrate on the handful that will directly apply in your first few months of training. The following are terms you'll need to know.

- **Rep.** The contraction or extension of a given muscle group against resistance, typically performed from a starting position of full extension to a finishing position of full contraction, and subsequent return to the starting position. We call a series of such movements, naturally enough, repetitions—from which we get the singular form, rep.
- **Set.** A collection of repetitions (anywhere from one to one hundred or more). Generally, a brief rest of thirty to ninety seconds is taken at the end of a set in order to catch one's breath and provide time for the muscle group involved in the set to partially recuperate. A typical routine calls for one to four sets of a given exercise to be performed.
- **Press.** Any form of pushing the resistance away from the body with either the arms or the legs.

- **Curl.** Any movement that involves pulling the resistance in toward the body with either the arms or the legs.
- **Clean.** No, this doesn't have anything to do with personal hygiene. Rather, it is the lifting of the barbell or dumbbell from the floor to the chest in one quick motion.
- **Poundage.** The amount of weight or resistance that you will be using in your exercises.
- **Limit weight.** The heaviest amount of resistance that you can lift for one repetition.
- **Routine.** The sum total of reps, sets, and exercises in any given workout or training session.

A BRIEF LESSON IN ANATOMY AND PHYSIOLOGY

Before you can effectively train your muscles, you need to know how they function so that you can select the exercises that will best stimulate them to grow. Without making this a complicated physiological dissertation, let's first examine a few of the body's basic structures and see how they work together—and how this knowledge will lead to your becoming a more informed and more successful bodybuilder.

- **Central nervous system.** The central nervous system is of vital importance to both the aspiring and competitive bodybuilder (as it is to the rest of our species and any other species). Without nerves, our bones wouldn't move, because our muscles wouldn't contract. The central nervous system consists of the spinal cord and the brain; it functions in conjunction with the peripheral nervous system, which comprises the ganglia and nerves that reside outside of the brain and spinal cord. The nervous system appears like thousands of little wires that function as transmitters, receivers, and interpreters of data from all parts of the body. It is responsible for stimulating the muscles of the body to contract, which in turn make it possible to move. Damage to the central nervous system, obviously, would impair the body's movement potential. Movement itself is accomplished when the nervous system stimulates the muscles, which then move the bones that support us via the tendinous attachments around our joints, which are connected by ligaments.
- **Ligaments.** Ligaments are fibrous bands that bind bone to bone. Their compactness determines to a large extent the flexibility of our joints. Great caution must be taken when you're training because if a ligament is stretched too far, the joint that it holds together will become loose, resulting in permanent damage to the tissue. (This is why some football players are never able to fully recover from serious knee injuries.) A joint that has been thusly injured will often "go out" without warning, due to the instability of its overstretched ligaments.

- **Tendons.** Tendons are the dense, fibrous bands at the end of muscles. Their function is to attach muscles to bones. Within the tendons are found the golgi tendon organs, whose function is to send signals to the brain to indicate stress and fatigue. Generally, the ache that you experience during strenuous exercise is being transmitted via the tendon and not the muscle.

- **Bones.** The human body contains 206 bones that, collectively, compose the skeleton. Muscles, as we have seen, are attached to bones by tendons and assist us in moving from one position to another.

- **Muscles.** There exist three distinct kinds of muscle tissue within the body: cardiac, skeletal, and smooth. Cardiac muscle is the heart, while smooth muscle assists organs such as the stomach and intestines in the passage and digestion of food. Skeletal muscle, on the other hand, is responsible for moving our bones. As

The human body has more than six hundred skeletal muscles, which accounts for our species' highly evolved dexterity and precision in movement.

we're looking to increase the size and strength of our skeletal muscles, it is to this group that we shall devote most of our attention. There are more than six hundred skeletal muscles, which yields a skeletal-muscle-to-bones ratio of almost three to one and accounts for our highly evolved dexterity and precision in movement.

In summary, nerves stimulate our muscles, which in turn move our bones via the tendinous attachments near joints, which are connected by ligaments. When functioning with its parts in proper unison, the body is an intricate and complex piece of machinery. Our objective as bodybuilders will be to increase the efficiency of our "machine" through regulated periods of stress, or tension, upon the muscles, tendons, and ligaments in order to have the central nervous system transmit the signal for "overcompensation," or muscle growth.

ANATOMY AND EXERCISE

When you're selecting exercises to perform for specific muscle groups, it's a definite asset to know the functions of the muscle structures you hope to involve. Table 1.1 is a brief list to assist you in the evaluation and selection process. This list is admittedly incomplete, but it should serve your purposes as a beginner because you will be concentrating solely on these muscle groups in order to build muscular mass. Use it as your base from which you can specialize on

TABLE 1.1 Muscle Structures, Functions, and Exercises

Vernacular	Muscle Group	Locale on Body	Function	Exercise
Extensors	Forearm extensors	Outer forearm	Open hand, extend wrist	Reverse wrist curls
Flexors	Forearm flexors	Inner forearm	Close hand, flex wrist	Wrist curls
Tris	Triceps	Back of upper arm	Extend forearm	Any presses, dips, or extension movements involving the arms
Bis	Biceps	Front of upper arm	Bend arm, supinate wrist	Curls
Brachy	Brachialis	Back of upper arm	Bend arm with wrist pronated	Reverse curls
Delts	Deltoids	Point of shoulder	Assist in raising upper arm	Lateral raises, elbows out to the sides
Pecs	Pectorals	Upper front of rib cage	Draw upper-arm bones toward each other	Bench presses, crossovers, flyes, pec deck
Traps	Trapezius	Upper back	Shrug shoulder	Shrugs
Abs	Rectus abdominus	Muscles of abdomen	Flex body at waist	Crunches
Obliques	External & internal obliques	Sides of waist	Rotate upper torso and bend torso to side	Side bends, obliques bends to the sides
Lats	Latissimus dorsi	Back muscles that impart V shape	Pull upper arm down and to the rear	Chins, rows, pull-downs
Quads	Quadriceps	Front of thigh	Straighten leg	Squats, leg presses, leg extensions
Hams	Hamstrings	Back of thigh	Bend leg	Leg curls, stiff-legged dead lifts

minor bodyparts when you reach a more advanced muscular state.

TRAINING PRINCIPLES

The vast majority of people who take up exercising with weights want to increase their present degree of muscle size. Unfortunately, enthusiasm can be the bodybuilder's worst enemy. Caught up in the throes of weight training, the aspiring trainee trains every day, performs as many sets as can be tolerated, and then wonders why progress, if it comes at all, does so at an unbelievably slow pace. While muscle growth is a slow process at the best of times, it doesn't have to be excessively slow, providing that you train properly. In fact, if you train exactly as I've outlined in this book, you'll be amazed at the transformation in your physique in just a matter of weeks. The reason is that weight training is powerful medicine that forces your body into a virtually instant response.

The harder you train, the faster your body overcompensates in the form of additional muscle mass, but also, the harder you train, the more rest and recuperation your body requires to bring about the physiological renovations in your physique. Therefore, your initial program will be based upon a three-day-per-week training schedule, which also happens to be among the top result-producing methods of bodybuilding. The legendary Steve Reeves utilized this method exclusively in building his incredible physique. Mike Mentzer, perhaps the greatest and most massively developed bodybuilder of all time, utilized a three-day-a-week routine right up until the day he won the 1976 Mr. America title.

In short, the three-day-per-week system works extremely well for beginners and is responsible for putting more muscle on more beginners than any other system of training in the world. Again, once you hit the intermediate stage, you will have to back off on the frequency a bit in order to allow your body ample time to produce the gains that your workouts have stimulated. Here are a few simple rules to follow that will help ensure your success.

1. Do *not* train more than three days a week.
2. Concentrate on each exercise you do; try to develop a mind-to-muscle link, whereby you are keenly aware of your muscles contracting against the resistance. Don't just start a set with the idea of simply getting the weight to the top using any means possible.
3. Don't "cheat" on an exercise. Don't utilize body swing or momentum to complete a contraction, no matter how difficult the exercise may become. Cheating increases momentum, which, in turn, diminishes muscular involvement in the exercise and, hence, reduces the exercise's productivity. Your goal is to involve as many muscle fibers as possible.
4. Your training days will be Monday, Wednesday, and Friday. Try not to

engage in anything too strenuous on your "off" days, as this would cut into your recovery ability, which should be utilized only to overcome the exhaustive effects of the weight-training workout. Performing other activities retards progress. If you miss a training day, don't panic and *don't* perform two workouts back-to-back thinking you can "make up" for it. Let it go—the extra recovery won't hurt your progress in the least— and might actually help it along.

5. Perform each movement slowly and under control to ensure that the muscle group you are training is doing all of the required work and that momentum is not involved. Remember this rule of thumb regarding velocity: Lift the weight in two seconds, hold it at the top for another two seconds, and then lower it in four seconds back to the starting position.

Because this will be the first time that you have trained on this program, weight training will represent a major shock to your physiological system. It is important that you understand this concept. It's the most intense form of exercise in existence, which is precisely why it produces such dramatic physiological results. Given these facts, doing more than the amount specified at this stage of your development is not at all desirable.

For this reason I recommend that, during your first month, you perform no more than one set of each exercise listed, and no more than two sets should be performed during month two. And now, on with the routine.

THE BASIC ROUTINE

Here's the routine in a nutshell:

1. Barbell squats:
   1 set of 15 reps

2. Pull-overs:
   1 set of 12 reps

3. Bench presses:
   1 set of 15 reps

4. Standing barbell presses:
   1 set of 10 reps

5. Bent-over barbell rows:
   1 set of 10 reps

6. Standing barbell curls:
   1 set of 10 reps

7. Stiff-legged dead lifts:
   1 set of 15 reps

8. Crunches:
   1 set of 20 reps

NOTE: The squats and pull-overs are to be performed back to back; as soon as you have finished your set of squats, rush to do your set of pull-overs.

Remember that this routine is to be performed on Mondays, Wednesdays, and Fridays. Under no circumstances should you attempt to get all three of the week's workouts in by training three days in a row! The alternate-day schedule is set up so for a reason: physiologists have determined that, unless you are a "natural" in the purest sense of the term (in which case you wouldn't need to worry about altering your appearance via weight training), your body needs approximately forty-eight hours of rest between workouts, both to recover from the training session and to allow the muscular subsystems to overcompensate in the form of increased muscle mass.

NOTE: Think of the formula this way: Train hard—rest a day to recover and grow; train hard—rest a day to recover and grow; train hard—rest for two days to recover and grow.

The details of how each exercise is to be performed are crucial. I've endeavored to make the descriptions as simple and comprehensive as possible because there are frequently three or four minor details that must be understood and followed. Read carefully every word of how the exercise is to be performed before attempting it. Your success depends almost exclusively upon the proper execution of the exercises in the routine. I've suggested moderate weights to start with, to ensure that correct form is employed during the performance of the exercise. Never complete a movement too rapidly, and make it as it should be—a muscular effort.

NOTE: Exercises that are new in each chapter offer detailed explanations and pictures that show you how to properly perform them. For performance review of repeated exercises, cross references are included so you can easily find the initial descriptions.

The Routine Explained

1. **Barbell squats:** Without question, squats are the top-ranked result-producing bodybuilding exercise. If you want to pack on pounds of solid muscle weight all over your physique, then give your all to squatting properly. And certainly this is the most effective leg building exercise that one can undertake with weights.

To perform the squat properly, stand erect with a barbell across your shoulders and take a deep breath. Now, with your lungs full, bend your knees and lower your body until you are in a full squat position; you should be slightly below a ninety-degree angle to your shins. As soon as you reach the bottom position, rise immediately—but under control—while at the same time expelling the air from your lungs, so that you will be ready for another intake of oxygen at the completion of the movement. Breathe in, and down you go for your second repetition, and so on until the required number of repetitions have been completed.

It is important to keep your head up at all times, and your chest should be held high. Some bodybuilders accomplish this by fixing

Barbell squat—Start position.

Barbell squat—Finish position.

their gaze on a spot two to three feet above eye level until the movement is finished. Also, some trainees prefer to perform squats with a small board under their heels to improve their balance. If you feel your balance is off somewhat, which it may be, owing to innate variations in bone structure, by all means utilize a board. Squats strongly affect the quadriceps, the four-headed muscle that makes up the bulk of the frontal thigh, the main action of which is to straighten the leg and to flex the hip.

As soon as you have completed your set of squats, you will immediately pick up a barbell and perform your second exercise, pull-overs. This immediate transfer from one exercise to another is known in body-building circles as a "superset," and you will be using it only for the first two exercises. Then you can take a sixty- to ninety-second breather.

2. Pull-overs: There's a twofold manner to developing a massive chest: one way is to develop the pectorals with exercises that build those muscles, and the other is to expand the rib cage with stretching exercises. Thus, performing both of these types of movements enlarges the chest's external musculature as well as its internal underpinnings.

Performance of the straight-arm pull-over is simple. Lie on a bench with a light barbell (or a centrally loaded dumbbell),

Dumbbell pull-over—Start position.

Dumbbell pull-over—Finish position.

held at arm's length over your chest. Maintaining the arm's-length position, slowly lower the weight until it almost touches the floor behind you. Make an effort to keep your arms locked throughout the movement, and when you inhale, attempt to draw in as much oxygen as you can while lifting the weight as high as possible. The weight is not a major factor in this exercise, whereas the degree of stretch most certainly is. A weight range of between ten and twenty pounds is recommended, dependent on your starting level of strength.

3. **Bench presses:** Because of the number of muscle groups that come into play (triceps, pectorals, deltoids, lats, etc.), the bench press is a great upper-body exercise. The main kinesiological function of the pectorals is to draw the arms into the midline of the body—or, more technically, to adduct the arms—so the action of the arms during the performance of the bench press closely parallels the pectorals' primary function. The bench press has its shortcomings, as you will learn further on, but for the beginner in search of overall muscle-mass increase, it's virtually the "perfect" exercise. It is a movement of great poundage potential, and this, combined with the fact that it stimulates a large group of muscles at one time (some more than others), makes it,

Barbell bench press—Start position.

Barbell bench press—Finish position.

like the squat, a tremendous weight-gaining exercise.

To perform the exercise properly, lie on a bench with a barbell at arm's length over your chest. Slowly lower the bar to your upper chest. Once the bar has touched your chest (I said "touched," not "bounced"; bouncing a weight accomplishes nothing but injury), slowly press it back up to the top position, and repeat the procedure for the required number of repetitions. Put the weight down, rest briefly, and then perform your next exercise.

4. Standing barbell presses: Whenever the average person asks you, "What can you lift?" chances are the question refers to this exercise. To the uninitiated, the standing barbell press is the touchstone of physical strength, and even experienced trainees place a lot of stock in evaluating one's strength by the performance of this exercise. Its status as an accurate gauge of individual strength is evidenced by its inclusion as one of the three Olympic lifts used in interna-

tional competition. The standing barbell press is an excellent deltoid developer. It also stimulates growth in the trapezius and, during its final stages, the triceps muscles.

In order to perform this exercise properly, you should clean (remember our definitions section earlier in the chapter) the barbell to your upper chest, or to the front of your shoulders. Then, slowly press the weight upward until your arms are fully extended over your head. Slowly lower the resistance back down to your shoulders (the starting position), and repeat the procedure for the required number of repetitions. Rest briefly, and then move on to your next exercise.

NOTE: When you're performing this exercise, there should be no assistance from the legs or excessive arching of the back. Sure, by using these little dodges you can hoist up a few more pounds—but that's not our objective here. We want the shoulders to receive the bulk of the stress and, consequently, the bulk of the muscle stimulation. Note that the bar should be cleaned

Standing barbell press—Midpoint position.

Standing barbell press—Finish position.

only once during each set, and that's at the beginning of the movement.

5. Bent-over barbell rows: It's always impressive to see well-developed upper-back muscles that fan out from the waist to the shoulders, giving the body that much sought-after V shape. One of the best upper-back exercises for developing that V shape is the bent-over barbell row. That's because the bulk of the stress of the barbell row is applied to the latissimus dorsi, which is the muscle responsible for the V shape. This is a large,

flat muscle whose Latin root means "broad of the back." Even though the latissimus dorsi, or lat muscles, are situated on the back, they are in effect arm muscles; their action is to draw the arm back behind the midline of the body and downward. In action, their movement resembles that of rowing a boat or climbing a rope.

To perform the barbell row, bend at the waist so that your torso is at a right angle (ninety degrees) to your legs. Grab hold of the bar so that your palms are facing your shins. Your hand spacing should be between

Barbell row—Start position.

Barbell row—Finish position.

two and two and a half feet. Slowly pull the bar up toward your torso until it touches your lower chest. From this fully contracted position, slowly lower the resistance back to the starting position (your arms should be fully extended), and repeat for the required number of repetitions. Rest briefly, and then perform your next exercise.

Remember that the barbell is to touch the floor only when the set is completed. This will ensure that maximum stimulation is imparted to the lats throughout the movement. Also remember to maintain the bent-over position throughout the set.

6. Standing barbell curls: This exercise involves the biceps and brachialis muscles of the upper arm. The biceps, on the front of the upper arm, lies on top of the brachialis and is responsible for supinating your wrist to a palms-up position and, in conjunction with the brachialis, flexes the elbow joint. In essence, this means that these muscles bend the arm, such as when you bring food to your mouth or hold a telephone receiver to your ear.

To perform the barbell curl, stand erect with a shoulder-width grip on the barbell and your palms facing front. Your arms should be fully extended so that the barbell is directly in front of your thighs. Now slowly lift, or curl, the barbell up to shoulder height, solely using the muscles of the upper arm by bending the elbows. From this fully contracted position, slowly lower the resistance back to the fully extended (or starting) position. Repeat for the required number of repetitions, and then rest briefly before performing your next exercise.

Remember to let only the upper arms do the work during this movement. Fight the

Standing barbell curl—Start position.

Standing barbell curl—Midpoint position.

Standing barbell curl—Finish position.

tendency to let additional muscle groups come into play by swinging the body or shrugging the shoulders to add momentum to the movement.

7. Stiff-legged dead lifts: This movement is a tremendous overall muscle developer and is also the single most productive exercise for the muscles of the lower back, referred to as the erector spinae muscles, which, as the name implies, act to keep the spine erect.

To perform the movement properly, stand erect with your feet just under the barbell. Then, by bending your knees, grasp the barbell, with your hands a little wider apart than shoulder width and your knuckles facing front. Now slowly begin to stand erect, straightening your legs as you do

so. Keep lifting the resistance until you're completely erect and the bar is in front of your thighs. Now slowly lower the resistance until it is back on the floor, and repeat the movement for the required number of repetitions. Rest briefly, and then move on to your next exercise.

Be sure to draw your shoulders well back at the completion of the movement in order to involve the trapezius muscle, which slopes down from your neck to your upper shoulders.

8. Crunches: This exercise strongly activates your abdominal muscles, which, when fully developed, really set off a well-muscled physique. How your abs appear, or even if they appear at all, is largely due to your dietary habits (an area we will concern

Stiff-legged dead lifts—Start position.

Stiff-legged dead lifts—Finish position.

ourselves with later). This means that no stomach exercise—repeat: no stomach exercise—will "melt" or "burn" or otherwise metamorphose bodyfat from your physique. Don't make the mistake of thinking that if you perform sit-up after sit-up, you will in some way be ridding your abdomen of surplus adipose; that's just not the way our species' physiology functions. Train hard to develop your stomach muscles, and then diet to reduce your subcutaneous bodyfat stores, and your abdominal muscles will stand out in bold relief.

Crunch—Finish position.

To perform crunches effectively, lie faceup on the floor—on a mat—with your hands behind your head. Try to keep your chin on your chest throughout the movement. Lift your feet up on top of a bench, with your legs slightly apart. From this starting position, slowly curl your trunk upward toward a sitting position. You'll find that you can accomplish a third of the required sit-up in this fashion, which is fine, because that is all the range of motion that your abdominals require to be stimulated into maximum growth. Once you have ascended to a fully contracted position, hold the position for a two-count, and then lower yourself slowly back to the starting position. Repeat for the required number of repetitions.

Concentrate and train hard during your first month on this program. You should notice a drastic difference at month's end after commencing this schedule and should be looking, and feeling, the better for it.

2

The Next Stage

After your first month of training, you should be noticing some substantial changes in both your physique and your health. You will have firmed up considerably; probably put on five to ten pounds, depending on your diet; and, for perhaps the first time in your life, become aware of numerous muscle groups throughout your body that spoke to you on the days after your training sessions with little twitches of pain. Not real pain, mind you, but a constant probing sort of sensation that let you know that some sort of activity—namely muscle stimulation—had occurred there only the day before. This is all to the good, as those twinges signified that you had stimulated some muscle growth, which is the reason you started bodybuilding in the first place.

Last month, on your beginner's program, you performed a total of one set per bodypart, trained three days a week, and used a predominantly straight-set approach—that is, you performed one set of a given exercise and then rested before moving on to a different movement.

During your second month of training, you will still train three days a week on alternate days, with weekends off, but you will be performing a total of three sets per bodypart and employing a method known as "forced reps." In this system you will never be performing more than five direct sets for any given bodypart, and even that maximum will occur only during periods of "specialization" on a muscle group that is lagging behind the others in development.

EXPANDING YOUR VOCABULARY

As just cited in the preceding section, the concept of specialization as it applies to bodybuilding will be new to you if you're a true neophyte. It is one of several additional "inside sports" terms that you will learn and employ during your second month of training.

Specialization

Although you are still a few months away from needing this concept, it will help you to learn it ahead of time for the purpose of developing a keener eye toward the assessment of your physique. Specialization simply means that your training becomes bodypart specific for a limited period. For instance,

if after training for a while, you notice that your arms are huge but your legs look like a television stand, thus throwing out your entire symmetry, you should elect to "specialize" on your legs in order to bring your overall appearance back into proper perspective. It's easy for one bodypart to overshadow another, and the earlier you can detect such an imbalance, the easier it will be for you to correct it.

Supersets

In supersetting, two separate exercises are performed back to back, with no resting whatsoever in between. You can rest for as long as is necessary after you have performed your superset cycle.

Forced Reps

Forced reps occur at the very end of your set, when you can no longer complete a full repetition. When you come to the point in an exercise (or, more technically, the point

Forced reps are a technique that helps to push your muscles to deeper levels of exhaustion.

in a set of an exercise) when you can no longer reach the fully contracted position, you have a partner, or "spotter," assist you in completing several additional repetitions by lifting some of the resistance for you. You're still attempting to complete the contraction yourself; your partner is providing as little help as is required for the rep to be completed.

Try to overcome the tendency to let your partner lift the weight for you. Even professional bodybuilders are sometimes inclined to take a "Thank God, you're here!" approach to forced reps, whereby the instant the partner starts to assist them in the movement, they drop their own involvement entirely. Sure, they grimace and groan and stamp their feet in an effort to hoodwink the partner into believing that they're really putting their last ounce of energy into the rep, but the poor training partner suddenly gets a hernia from assuming the full brunt of raising the resistance at a mechanically disadvantageous position. When you see your training partner preparing to give you some forced reps, your *last* thought should be, "Thank God you're here!"

A forced-reps set is brutally hard and should have you wishing your partner were suddenly out of town, or anywhere other than in the gym with you. The fact that forced reps will make your exercises so much more intense and, consequently, so much more demanding is why the technique is so effective in stimulating phenomenal muscle growth. Keep in mind this maxim, which

was taught to me by legendary bodybuilder Mike Mentzer: The harder you train, the faster you'll grow! This truism will serve you well your entire training life.

As just discussed, a *spotter* is simply a training partner or friend who assists you. Whenever someone stands behind you to make sure that the weight you're bench-pressing doesn't pin you to the bench, or assists you in completing your repetitions, the person is said to be "spotting" you.

A COMMENT ABOUT DIET

One of the biggest misconceptions in bodybuilding today is the fallacy that you must ingest a magical combination of vitamins, minerals, and protein supplements in order to build large muscles. While I'll discuss the issue of nutrition as it applies to muscle building and fat loss in Chapter 16, I'd like to touch on a few dietary facts here and now.

First of all, if building muscle were as easy as taking a supplement, then training would be obsolete. The fact that you cannot "eat your way to a great physique" should be self-evident, but aspiring bodybuilders nevertheless spend thousands of dollars on supplements that do little else than enrich the color of their urine. Blunt, yes, but true! Diet in the beginning stages of bodybuilding is anything but complicated: if you want to get bigger, which is usually the motivation behind initiating a bodybuilding program, then you should train hard and eat lots. Pure and simple, eat anything you want, whenever you want; just make sure that you are eating a balanced diet. It serves your body-building program little good if you consume food from a diet that is lopsided in regard to any of the macronutrients (for example, fats, proteins, or carbohydrates). Eat the bulk of your foods in a more or less balanced fashion. In fact, tip the scale, if at all, in favor of carbohydrates, since they provide the fuel for all your weight-training sessions as well as being the primary energy source of your brain. Given that carbohydrates also are encased in foodstuffs that happen to taste the best (pasta, bread, sugar, fruits, etc.), it's usually not a burden to consume ample quantities of them.

If you've undertaken bodybuilding to lose fat, as opposed to weight—there is a major distinction—simply reduce your food intake slightly. I say "slightly" because drastic caloric reduction causes the body to actually slow down its metabolism in anticipation of a scarcity of food. This, of course, is counter-productive to what you wish to accomplish.

The most effective route to fat loss, then, is to train intensely to stimulate muscle growth (the routines I'll provide are designed to do just that) and reduce your food intake slightly—say, 500 calories below what would otherwise be necessary to main-tain your present bodyweight. Again, keep your diet balanced or tipped in favor of the carbohydrate element, and you'll notice a consistent level of fat loss while at the same time increasing your muscle-mass ratio.

The combination of these two factors will create a dramatic difference in the appear-ance of your physique and create a base of health and vitality that will be all but impenetrable throughout your life.

THE ROUTINE

This month we're going to alter our routine marginally by adding in some new exercises and subtracting a few from last month. The reason we will be switching exercises occasionally is to avoid both mental and physical staleness, the inevitable result of engaging in unaltered activities for prolonged periods. Some of the exercises, such as squats, will remain in our program due to their intrinsic value as proven muscle builders.

1. Barbell squats:
   3 sets of 15 reps
   Supersetted with . . .

2. Pull-overs:
   3 sets of 15 reps

3. Upright barbell rows:
   3 sets of 12 reps
   Supersetted with . . .

4. Bench presses:
   3 sets of 10–15 reps

5. Presses behind the neck:
   3 sets of 12 reps

6. Standing dumbbell curls:
   1 set of 15 reps, 2 sets of 10 reps
   Supersetted with . . .

7. **Lying triceps extensions:**
1 set of 15 reps, 2 sets of 10 reps

8. **Stiff-legged dead lifts:**
3 sets of 15 reps

The Routine Explained

1. **Barbell squats:** Stand erect with a barbell across your shoulders and take a deep breath. Now, with your lungs full, bend your knees and lower yourself slowly, in four seconds, and then ascend in two seconds back to the starting position for the required number of repetitions. See Chapter 1 for a full description of this exercise and its benefits. Superset with . . .

2. **Pull-overs:** Lie on a bench with a light barbell (or a centrally loaded dumbbell), which should be held at arm's length over your chest. Maintaining the arm's-length position, slowly lower the weight until it almost touches the floor behind you. Make an effort to keep your arms locked throughout the movement, and when you inhale, attempt to draw in as much oxygen as you can while lifting the weight as high as possible. The weight is not a major factor in this exercise, whereas the degree of stretch most certainly is. A weight range of between ten and twenty pounds is recommended, dependent on your starting level of strength. Remember to slowly lower the weight as far behind you as possible and also pull it over your chest in a slow and deliberate fashion. See Chapter 1 for a full description of this exercise and its benefits.

3. **Upright barbell rows:** This is an excellent exercise for both your trapezius and deltoid (shoulder) muscles. Place your hands about six inches apart on a barbell with an overhand grip (your palms should be facing your thighs). Keeping your body straight and stationary, slowly pull the weight up to your clavicles (collar bone). Keep the barbell in close, and then slowly, in four seconds, lower it back to the starting position. Remember that your development will be accelerated if you work your muscles in both the upward and downward portions of the exercise. Repeat the movement for three sets of twelve repetitions. Supersetted with . . .

Upright barbell row—Finish position.

Bench press—Finish position. Make sure your partner assists you just enough to make the last few reps possible—not to make it easier for you.

4. **Bench presses:** Use the same style as described in Chapter 1, but don't be afraid to really push for those last few reps during your third set. Your partner should assist you just enough to allow you to complete your repetitions—not to make the exercise easier for you! Be sure to concentrate fully during both the raising (positive) and the lowering (negative) portions of the movement.

5. **Presses behind the neck:** Use the same form as outlined in Chapter 1 for the standing barbell press. It's not necessary to clean the weight here; note the seated starting position in the photo as an alternative technique. Begin with a light poundage in order to warm up your entire shoulder girdle. Take a deep breath before pressing the weight up smoothly to the fully extended position of your arms, and then lower the resistance twice as slowly (four seconds) back to the starting position. Add weight to the bar (approximately 20 percent more than your warm-up weight) and perform two more sets.

You may notice that you will not be as strong in this movement as you were last month. The reason for this isn't that you're becoming weaker, but rather that your last four exercises have involved your deltoids to a greater extent, and consequently, your shoulder muscles are more fatigued than they were when you performed this exercise last month. Battle through the fatigue to get your prescribed number of repetitions, all the while maintaining perfect form.

Press behind the neck—Start position.

Press behind the neck—Finish position.

6. Standing dumbbell curls: These next two exercises are to be performed in a superset. First, to perform the standing dumbbell curls, grab a pair of dumbbells and hold them at your sides with the palms touching your upper thighs. Slowly curl both arms up until the dumbbells are at shoulder level. Pause briefly in this fully contracted position, and then lower the dumbbells slowly, in four seconds, back to the starting position. Perform your first set as a slow, controlled, warm-up set (supersetted with the next exercise), and then increase the resistance by 20 percent (give or take a couple of pounds, depending on your existing strength levels) and superset your next two sets for 10 repetitions each. Supersetted with . . .

Lying triceps extension—Start position.

7. Lying triceps extensions: Lie on an exercise bench, holding a barbell (or E-Z curl bar) in both hands directly over your chest. From this position, slowly lower the resistance, in four seconds, to a point just behind your head. From this fully extended position, slowly press the resistance back up to the starting position. Just as in the preceding exercise, use your first set as a slow, controlled, warm-up set, and then add approximately 20 percent more to the bar and perform two more sets (supersetted with the previous exercise) of 10 repetitions.

8. Stiff-legged dead lifts: A version of this exercise was described in the previous chapter, and both are among the best total-body exercises. They not only work your lower back but also place considerable stress on your forearms, biceps, lats, shoulders, and trapezius muscles.

Using an over-under grip whereby one palm is facing your thighs while the other palm is facing away, grab hold of a moder-

Standing dumbbell curl—Finish position.

ately weighted barbell and, with your arms straight, stand upright so that the bar is resting across the front of your thighs and your back is straight. From this position, slowly, in four seconds, lower the resistance to the floor, making sure to keep your legs locked straight (as opposed to the previous dead lift exercise, in which you began with bent knees and then straightened). Because of the nature of this exercise, it's not necessary to use a lot of weight. You don't want to strain your lower back; you simply want to concentrate on stimulating the muscles that support it. Repeat for the required number of sets and repetitions.

Again, you should train on three alternate days per week. The workouts will stimulate muscle growth, while your days off allow that growth to take place. Muscle growth is a slow process, contingent solely upon the intensity levels that you are willing and able to generate in your training sessions. So, train hard, eat a balanced diet that is modified to suit your objectives, and rest to recover and grow, and by the end of this month you'll notice a substantial muscle-mass increase—which, of course, you'll need before proceeding to the workouts outlined in Chapter 3, "Fewer Sets + More Reps = More Mass!"

3

Fewer Sets + More Reps = More Mass!

By this time in your training, you should have noticed some spectacular changes in both your health and physique. Your chest should be deeper, your back wider, your shoulders broader, and your arms and legs fuller—that is, if you've been following my instructions to the letter.

If you haven't yet realized these results, go back and reread the introductory chapters carefully and run through the routines again. Believe me, they will work when applied properly!

One of the biggest disappointments shared by many people, regardless of age, who take up the science of bodybuilding is that they never seem to gain "fast enough." Almost everybody who has ever attended a Mr. Olympia contest wants to look—immediately—like the competitors seen on stage. To this end some people even copy the champions' precontest training routines in a misguided effort to somehow hasten this

Genetics is the prime determinant of how large an individual's muscles will become. While training can help maximize one's potential for muscle size, genetics sets the limits on how big one can ultimately get.

transformational process. After all, it worked for the champions, right? Wrong!

I've stated this before, but it bears repeating: the champions are the thoroughbreds of our species; it's in their genes—or, more specifically, it's in their muscle bellies—to be big musclemen. Their physiques are inordinate due to their being genetically predisposed to carry a large musculature on their frames, and not because of any "magic" to be found within their training routines (e.g., triple split; push/pull; intensity or insanity—I love that one!; up and down the rack; twenty sets per bodypart) or their secret dietary methods.

It's time we, as a group, woke up to the fact that it's not in the genetic cards for all of us to be massively muscled. Nor can we alter our reality by simply aping the training routine of a certain champion. In fact, the champion's training routine, particularly his precontest routine, would have about as much bearing on our attaining his muscle size as would our wearing the same shoes as he does.

Remember this point: the first rule of success in bodybuilding is to work within our genetic framework. Without this principle, most of the other rules have no application. Moreover, given the level of drugs that most of the champion bodybuilders take, probably very few of the rules that govern human physiology have much bearing on them. The drugs alter human physiology into something foreign to our species. Once these drugs enter the equation, and by drugs I specifically refer to steroids here, the act of emulating the training methods of the bodybuilder you see on stage becomes pointless. The muscles of steroid users no longer create the same amount of waste by-products, nor do they fatigue at the same rate; drugs have altered both processes beyond the confines of simple human physiology. Suffice it to say that unless you currently are on steroids, or are resolved to use them regardless of the potential consequences, you'll experience little, if any, gains in muscle mass by training like the champions.

Natural muscular gains come when you train intelligently, which means observing and understanding the economics of growth and recovery.

DECEPTIVE CLAIMS

Bodybuilding, like most other human endeavors, has had and continues to have its share of bizarre and fantastic claims, generally made by people who are every bit as extraordinary as the claims they advance. As you are now entering your third month, it's important that you be informed of just what deception awaits you on your journey to physical "perfection" at this point in your training. Armed with this knowledge in advance, you will be better able to recognize and avoid fast-talkers who would have you believe and support baseless and potentially harmful training, nutritional, and, most important, cognitive practices.

The most common error that you'll encounter is the "visualization" or cognitive "mind over matter" arguments, replete with similes that involve *biceps like mountains*, *backs like manta rays*, or similar nonsense. These are, in effect, mind-over-genetics arguments, or what the late philosopher-novelist Ayn Rand would have called the "I Wish versus It Is" polemic. This premise, in essence, instructs you to ignore the fact that you are only five foot two and have brown eyes, because, by God, if you really want to be six foot six and have eyes of blue, then all you have to do is *believe that it's possible—* and it will happen!

The proponents of such irrational gibberish have their own nomenclature that features constructs such as "mental imagery" and, of course, "visualization"—and it's rampant throughout bodybuilding. Statements such as "Believe and Achieve" adorn the back of many a personally inscribed weight belt. This is chicanery

The fact that an individual has huge arms doesn't mean that it was the training methods that were responsible for building them.

straight out of *The Flim-Flam Man*. It won't put another inch on your arms, no matter how Cartesianly clear and distinct your "mystical" mental processes and thoughts about the size of your muscles may be. I mean, go ahead—envision your biceps the size of Mount Everest. Give me a call when they reach 29,028 feet above sea level. It's exactly the same logic as if I were to claim that I could leap over an apartment complex; you'd be justified in thinking me deluded, regardless of how firmly I held to the vividness of the fantasy.

Likewise, if a bodybuilder of international repute should tell you that he has peaks on his biceps because he envisioned them as miniature mountains, and not because genetics put an egg on his biceps the day his DNA took hold, you should be equally suspect about his cognitive faculties.

Nevertheless, such claims are made almost daily regarding the mystical import of the "mind" in training. Sure, the mind is important; without it you couldn't even tie your shoes, let alone engage in barbell training, but it's not nearly as omnipotent as some "authorities" would have you believe.

The mind is important in keeping you motivated to get into the gym and train intensely enough to stimulate your muscles to grow. As I conceded earlier, this training routine is not an easy one to adopt for the long term. In fact, it's downright uncomfortable—so much so that anyone who feels the inclination to engage in visualization or cognitive gymnastics involving mountain-peak biceps, manta-ray lats, or fluffy clouds really isn't training. The person is simply going through the motions and relaxing, because relaxation, or sleep, is the time we are best able to engage in such flights of fancy. (We just refer to them as dreams.)

And if such people also exhibit impressive physiques, it's only further testimony to the supreme role that genetics played in their physical development—as opposed to their mystical thought processes and inefficient training methods.

TRAINING

If genetics, then, is the be-all and end-all of bodybuilding, and you're not the spitting image of Conan the Barbarian at the moment, should you just throw in the towel and write it off to a bad deal of the genetic cards? By no means! The fact that you don't have the muscle bellies of an Arnold Schwarzenegger or Mike Mentzer doesn't mean that you don't have the genetics of an equally impressive *you* when developed to the uppermost limits of your potential. After all, Steve Reeves, Arnold Schwarzenegger, Mike Mentzer, Lou Ferrigno, Bruce Lee, Mike Tyson, and Lee Labrada didn't have identical genetics, and yet all went on to develop very impressive (and very muscular) physiques.

If you train properly, you can realize your own unique physiological potential, which may even supersede any of the competitors on the Mr. Olympia stage today! What, then, is "proper" training? Simply put, proper training involves stimulating muscle growth and then allowing your body sufficient time to realize that growth once it's been stimulated.

To accomplish this, your workouts must be intense, and since intensity and duration exist in inverse proportion to one another, your workouts must also be brief. The more intense the workouts, the greater the muscle stimulation, and the briefer the workouts must be.

One other factor that enters into this workout equation is recovery. This falls into the "off" time you have in between your workouts. My staff and I have conducted a series of tests and studies regarding this phenomenon at our Nautilus North fitness center and have concluded that once you get stronger, it will take you approximately three days to recover the energy you expended during your workout. It will then take you another three to four days to overcompensate, or grow bigger. In other words, as you grow stronger, you will require a full seven days off between workouts to allow the muscle you stimulated in your workout to grow.

As explained in Chapter 1, while you are still a beginner, you must have at least two days of rest between high-intensity training sessions, and more if you're exceptionally strong. With any less than this amount, you'll not progress at all, and you may even begin to regress. So, first train hard to stimulate growth, which means that your workouts must be of brief duration (no more than thirty to forty-five minutes per workout), and rest afterward for a minimum of forty-eight hours. If these precepts are followed, you will grow progressively larger muscles with every visit to the gym.

THE ROUTINE

1. Barbell squats:
   1 × 20 reps

2. Chin-ups:
   1 × maximum reps

3. Seated barbell presses:
   1 × 12 reps

4. Bent-over barbell rows:
   1 × 12 reps

5. Dumbbell flyes:
   1 × 12 reps

6. Upright barbell rows:
   1 × 12 reps

7. Incline dumbbell curls:
   1 × 12 reps

8. Seated French presses:
   1 × 12 reps

9. Stiff-legged dead lifts:
   1 × 20 reps

10. Crunches:
   1 × 15 reps

11. Wrist curls:
   1 × 15 reps

12. Hammer curls:
   1 × 12 reps

The Routine Explained

1. Barbell squats: Stand erect with a barbell across your shoulders and take a deep breath. Now, with your lungs full, bend your knees and lower your body until you are in a full squat position; you should be slightly below a ninety-degree angle to your shins. As soon as you reach the bottom position, rise immediately—but under control—while at the same time expelling the air from your lungs, so that you will be ready for another intake of oxygen at the completion of the movement. Breathe in, and down you go for your second repetition, and so on until the required number of repetitions have been completed. See Chapter 1 for a full description of this exercise and its benefits.

2. Chin-ups: Chin-ups, like squats, also work several muscle groups, thereby stimulating significant overall muscle growth. To begin, grasp the chin-up bar with a palms-up grip. (You may require straps to reinforce your grip for the required number of repetitions.) Slowly begin to contract the muscles in your arms, and try to touch the bar to your lower chest when you have reached the apex of your ascent. Hold this contracted position for a two-count, and then lower yourself slowly (four seconds) back to the starting position, all the while making sure that the latissimus dorsi muscles are constantly contracted. Repeat this procedure until at least eight repetitions have been completed.

Chin-up—Finish position.

Chin-up—Start position.

If you can't perform a chin-up on your own, you may either use an assisted chin-up machine, if your local gym has one, or do a negative-only set. We'll discuss negatives further in the next chapter, but for now, here's what to do: Stand on a chair facing the chin-up bar, grab the bar, and step off. Under full muscle control, lower yourself to a stretched position as slowly as you can. Repeat to exhaustion. When you can complete ten negatives, you should be able to perform at least three or four regular chin-ups.

3. Seated barbell presses: This exercise is performed in the same manner as the standing barbell presses described in

Seated barbell press—Finish position.

spacing should be between two and two and a half feet. Slowly pull the bar up toward your torso until it touches your lower chest. From this fully contracted position, slowly lower the resistance back to the starting position (your arms should be fully extended), and repeat for the required number of repetitions. Rest briefly, and then perform your next exercise. See Chapter 1 for a full description and the benefits of this exercise.

Chapter 1. This time you will perform them seated. Some gyms have a special bench with supports to take the weight from. If you do not have access to such a bench, simply clean the barbell to your shoulders and sit down on a flat bench and begin the exercise.

4. Bent-over barbell rows: To perform the barbell row, bend at the waist so that your torso is at a right angle (ninety degrees) to your legs. Grab hold of the bar so that your palms are facing your shins. Your hand

5. Dumbbell flyes: Grab two fairly heavy dumbbells (remember that "heavy" is relative) and lie faceup on a bench. Slowly lower the dumbbells from an overhead position in an outward arc until they are a bit below chest level. Pause for one or two seconds, and then begin to slowly raise the dumbbells back to the starting overhead position in the same outward arc. (The movement should resemble your hugging a barrel.)

6. Upright barbell rows: Place your hands about six inches apart on a barbell with an

Bent-over barbell row—Start position.

Bent-over barbell row—Finish position.

Dumbbell flye—Start position.

Dumbbell flye—Finish position.

overhand grip (your palms should be facing your thighs). Keeping your body straight and stationary, slowly pull the weight up to your clavicles (collar bone). Keep the barbell in close, and then slowly, in four seconds, lower it back to the starting position. See Chapter 2 for a full description and the benefits of this exercise.

7. **Incline dumbbell curls:** Take hold of two dumbbells and sit down on an incline bench (preferably an incline of 45 degrees). With your arms extended and your palms facing each other, slowly curl your arms up until your biceps are fully contracted, making sure to turn both palms up at the top of the curl. Pause briefly, and then lower both arms back to the start position. Repeat for 12 repetitions.

8. **Seated French presses:** While dips are arguably the best triceps exercise, your chest and delts may be too fatigued at this stage to allow you to train your triceps adequately. Not to worry. The seated French press is a great triceps-isolation exercise. To perform

Upright barbell row—Finish position.

this exercise properly, grab hold of a Triceps Blaster (I know, I hate the name too!) or an E-Z curl bar. Press the weight overhead as if you were about to perform the press behind the neck. Now, instead of lowering your elbows, keep them stationary (beside your ears) and lower only your forearms, until they are as far down toward the center of

Incline dumbbell curl—Start position.

Incline dumbbell curl—Finish position.

Seated French press—Start position.

Seated French press—Finish position.

your back as they can go. The time structure is the same with this exercise: two seconds up and four seconds down. Repeat for 12 repetitions.

9. Stiff-legged dead lifts: Using an over-under grip whereby one palm is facing your thighs while the other palm is facing away, grab hold of a moderately weighted barbell and, with your arms straight, stand upright so that the bar is resting across the front of your thighs and your back is straight. From this position, slowly, in four seconds, lower the resistance to the floor, making sure to keep your legs locked straight. See Chapters 1 and 2 for variations on this exercise.

10. Crunches: To perform crunches effectively, lie faceup on the floor with your hands behind your head. Try to keep your chin on your chest throughout the movement. Keep your feet on the floor, with your knees slightly open. From this starting position, slowly curl your trunk upward toward a sitting position. You'll find that you can accomplish a third of the required sit-up in this fashion, which is fine, because that is all the range of motion that your abdominals require to be stimulated into maximum growth. Once you have ascended to a fully contracted position, hold the position for a two-count, and then lower yourself slowly back to the starting position. See Chapter 1 for a full description of this exercise.

Crunch—Start position.

Crunch—Finish position.

11. Wrist curls: Take hold of a barbell in both hands, with your palms facing forward (as you would if performing a standing barbell curl), and sit on the end of a bench. Lift the barbell so that your forearms are resting across the tops of your thighs and the barbell is over the ends of your knees. Slowly lower your wrists until they are fully extended. From this position, slowly curl your wrists upward as far as they can go. Pause briefly in this fully contracted position, and then lower the bar back down until your wrists are fully extended again.

Wrist curl—Start position.

Wrist curl—Finish position.

12. Hammer curls: While standing, grab a pair of dumbbells and hold them at your sides. Your palms should be facing in toward your hips. Slowly, making sure to maintain the same palm position, curl one dumbbell up toward your shoulder, while the other stays at your side. Pause briefly in the position of full contraction, and then slowly lower the dumbbell back to the starting position. As soon as that dumbbell is back in the starting position, slowly curl the dumbbell in the opposite arm up to a position of full contraction, while the other arm is held down at your side.

SETS

The question of what is the "ideal" number of sets to perform for a bodypart is an area of bodybuilding that is a gray fog at the best of times. Certainly, twenty sets per bodypart, regardless of the bodypart, is not only unnecessary but also counterproductive. Reducing that number to half—ten sets—would seem to be a step in

Hammer curl—Start position (right arm).

Hammer curl—Finish position (right arm).

Hammer curl—Start position (left arm).

Hammer curl—Start position (left arm).

the right direction. However, an examination of the available literature in the world of science reveals that maximum strength and muscle-mass increases can be obtained from one set of an exercise and that additional sets yield no appreciable difference. You can do additional sets if you like, but don't for a minute believe that you're stimulating greater size and strength gains by doing so.

The proviso with the one-set method is that the set has to be taken to the point of "failure"—the point in a set at which an additional rep is impossible despite your greatest effort. Your training up until now has involved two sets during specialization periods, and you've made progress. That progress is exactly the reason why you must now reduce your training volume if you hope to progress further.

It's a well-documented fact that the average individual has the potential to increase his or her starting level of strength by at least 300 percent. However, that same individual's recovery ability has the potential to increase by only 50 percent. This means that the stronger you become, the greater the likelihood of overtraining becomes, unless you taper off the volume of your training sessions accordingly.

This routine will consist of reducing your training volume by approximately two-thirds. Don't be misled into thinking that briefer training is easier. Remember the nature of intensity: the harder you train, the briefer must be the duration of your workout. This workout will be hard—brutally so—and you'll progress as at no other time in your training career as a result of it. The repetition guidelines are the upper end of the scale; when you can successfully reach these integers, increase the resistance by 5 percent and try to reach these repetitions all over again. Also remember to take each set to muscular failure, and lift the weight in perfect form. That is, take two to five seconds to raise the resistance and four seconds to lower it.

Utilize this program on a two-day-per-week basis (for example, Mondays and Thursdays), and use your off days for rest and recovery—and watch yourself grow!

4

What About Steroids?

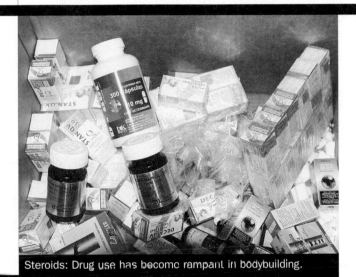

Steroids: Drug use has become rampant in bodybuilding.

A chapter issuing a note of caution is in order before we move on to Part 2. While the primary focus of this book is training, at this point I want you to clearly understand what role, if any, anabolic steroids play in building muscle and why they pose a health risk, so we can put the topic behind us.

Bear in mind that steroids don't represent the whole of bodybuilding drugs and are only one class of such substances. However, steroids are so much in the public eye these days that they warrant a preliminary presentation devoted to what they are, what they do, what they don't do, and whether their supposed benefits outweigh their obvious risks.

TWO CLASSES OF BODYBUILDERS

In the course of my career as a bodybuilding journalist, I came to be disabused of a great deal of my naïveté about the sport—or so I thought, until one memorable day. During an interview for an article, I casually asked a bodybuilder what drugs he took in preparation for a contest. In response, he picked up a pen and proceeded to write out a laundry list of substances, including Dianabol, Clembuteral, Halotestin, Fastin, and others— noting whether each was taken daily, every other day, during the off-season, or right before an event.

The roster he provided stunned me. Despite my supposed enlightenment, I still believed that bodybuilding was about training intelligently and building the body through scientific dietary practices. Evidently, though, there are two classes of body-builders: "real" and "professional." The real bodybuilders are from the old school and develop hard, honest muscle through their efforts in the gym. Far too many professional bodybuilders compose the other class. They inject all sorts of bizarre substances into their bodies, causing their muscles to become swollen or "puffy," and they are paid big money to risk their lives to look this way.

Small wonder that most of the body-builders who are heavy drug users end up looking like hell. The vast majority of the competitors of the 1970s and '80s have suffered serious coronary problems and/or look as if they never touched a weight in their lives. Some look considerably older and worse for wear than most beginners to the sport. Contrast that camp with champions such as Steve Reeves, John Grimek, Reg Park, and Larry Scott. This is not to suggest that none of these four knew what testosterone was (although both Reeves and Grimek denied ever using steroids to me personally), but even if they did elect that route at times, the doses were so minuscule as to be negligible in comparison with what is going on today.

It's no secret that anabolic steroids abound in the sport of bodybuilding, not to mention most other professional sports, including baseball. Many champions won't train unless they are on "roids," "the sauce," "the juice," or whatever hip label they apply. Some swear that you can't expect to compete without them, and some have recently gone to jail for peddling them to aspiring body-builders just like you!

That "juice" has been with us, in greater or lesser amounts, for decades. After the 1988 Olympic Games fiasco in Seoul with Canadian sprinter Ben Johnson's positive test following his (rescinded) world-record 100-meter-run performance, Canada became synonymous with steroid use in the eyes of its international peers. Then, after a series of drug tests at the Arnold Schwarzenegger Classic in Columbus, Ohio, in 1990, body-builders from the United States, Lebanon, and West Germany were also indicted for steroid use.

Does this scenario imply that everyone in the sports of track-and-field and bodybuilding is on anabolic steroids? No, but it does mean that athletes will now have to seriously calculate the consequences of using the drugs should they be caught—and with effective drug tests they probably will get caught. (I say "probably" because most athletes know ways to beat the tests.) A more urgent question is, will the athletes who use anabolic agents cause irreparable damage to their bodies or, perhaps, die from their ingestion? This is where the picture becomes very murky indeed.

The issue of whether steroids are as dangerous as some reports allege rests largely upon the individual response and dosage. This leads us to the exploration of just what anabolic steroids are and how this whole mess got started.

THE ORIGINS OF ANABOLIC STEROIDS

Anabolic steroids are synthetic derivatives of the male sex hormone testosterone. There are two components to any male sex hormone: androgenic and anabolic. The former refers to the masculinizing effects, such as facial hair, deepening of the voice, and aggressiveness, while the latter refers exclusively to the drug's tissue-building properties.

Anabolic steroids have been described as the "scourge of bodybuilding"—ironically, by a bodybuilder who later developed severe gynecomastia (a condition, resulting from steroid use, that develops breast tissue in males). (Who ever said that to be a bodybuilder, one must first renounce hypocrisy?)

Several international medical societies and sports organizations have also taken strong positions against steroid use, citing what they deem to be unsportsmanlike conduct and health hazards. This message, however, is ambiguous on both fronts. First off, competitors in a sport are expected to direct all of their energy toward being successful in their objective, and the use of steroids is viewed by many members of the athletic community as simply another means toward the attainment of this end. Meanwhile, the health-hazard threat has not been backed up conclusively, owing to a paucity of long-term experimentation in a controlled environment.

Athletes taking drugs is certainly nothing new. In 1879, the famous Six-Day Cycle Races were held for the first time, and even then, the coaches and trainers were known as drug mixers and "medicators" and were mixing some fairly potent potions— primarily derivatives of cocaine and heroin.

The term *doping* first appeared in English dictionaries around 1889 and referred to a mixture of opium and other narcotics used for horses. The root word can be traced to a Dutch word *dop*, which was a beverage given to Zulu warriors prior to battle. The word was subsequently adopted into the Boer language, and an *e* was eventually tacked on, resulting in *dope*—the slang term for drugs that is still in use today.

Regarding the activities and properties of androgens, some connection between the body's muscle mass and the activity of androgens had at least been suspected by the medical community for many years. The limited muscular development of eunuchs, for example, has been known since antiquity.

The first real report on the effects of androgens injected intramuscularly was the Borgrows report of 1981, which revealed that protein was spared when synthetic hormones were injected. Forty-six years prior to this, German physicists had discovered that pure crystalline hormone could be both isolated from testicular material and synthesized in a test tube.

The research of these and other scientists allowed relatively safe steroids to be marketed to the general public, meaning people who had a legitimate need for these substances. These initial steroids were never intended for healthy people! In the Second World War they were used for the treatment of burn victims specifically because of their tissue-building, or "anabolic," properties. They were also employed by the various hospitals in order to treat patients who, for whatever reason, were unable to manufacture their own testosterone and consequently lacked the benefit of the hormone's androgenic properties, the male secondary sexual characteristics necessary for normal and complete physical development.

It wasn't long afterward that athletes, hearing of the drugs' muscle-building properties, decided that since the male sex hormone testosterone was responsible for the development of sex characteristics such as increased musculature and reduced adipose storage, it followed that by increasing the ratio of testosterone within their own bodies, they would achieve a corresponding increase in their muscle size and strength. That would be a definite plus for their athletic endeavors. Ben Johnson is proof that, on the surface, their assumptions were correct. Bodybuilders in particular exploited this new drug. There are accounts of bodybuilders using steroids for the purpose of increasing their muscle mass as far back as the late 1940s.

THE SIDE EFFECTS

The bodybuilder who considers using steroids is immediately faced with an ethical decision: is the end really going to justify the means? Does a moment of fame and a medal really compensate for possible liver impairment, heart disorders, and sterility? The attitude of athletes is already well known: for the most part, they develop a tunnel vision about victory; they feel they *must* win—at any price. What is less known is what price this attitude carries with it in terms of the physical and often mental aberrations that can be engendered by anabolic ingestion.

Since steroids act directly upon the nervous system, your personality—being a product of your nervous system—is the first noticeable area of change. The many psychological symptoms noted while people are on steroid therapy range from fluctuating libido to headaches, lethargy, and aggression. Research also reveals that these side effects are dose related and are reversible on cessation of the drug.

The physiological effects are much more dramatic. In the literature published by ParkeDavis Pharmaceuticals about its steroid Adroyd, the information pertaining to dosage and administration takes up little more than one paragraph, whereas the information pertaining to "potential side effects" runs to ten paragraphs! The reactions listed include hepatitis and temporary sterility in males and include hirsutism, menstrual irregularities, and male-pattern baldness in females. Again, the literature points out that most of these conditions are contingent on dosage and duration of steroid therapy and are usually reversible on cessation of the drug.

REALITY

The reality of the situation is that steroids, like most other things, have the potential to do the user much harm if they either are abused or are ingested by someone who is genetically susceptible to certain medical conditions such as liver tumors and heart disease. That detail alone should give one pause. The central problem is that an accurate assessment of how steroids will affect you can be made only in retrospect, and by then it might be too late. Too little is known of both the effects and the side effects of steroids to make experimenting on yourself and becoming an anabolic guinea pig worth the risk.

Besides, take a gander at the sort of physique that anabolic steroids produce and ask yourself if looking bloated and undergoing frequent liver, blood, and serum testosterone tests (a regular battery is recommended for steroid users) and footing a monthly bill of $300 really justifies the final result. (That dollar figure, by the way, is low. I know of a Masters Mr. Olympia competitor who spent upward of $80,000 in anabolics while preparing for the contest.) Then look at the physique of Steve Reeves, with his flawless proportions and bona fide, drug-free, eighteen-and-a-half-inch arms, which he obtained by training properly. To my mind, there's no comparison. (See, you've already saved yourself a minimum of $3,600 a year!)

All this is not to take anything away from our current crop of champions. I just think that they would look much better than they currently do if they dropped the synthetic chemicals that have altered their appearance into something other than human and tried instead to look the best they can with their own natural human physiologies via proper training.

Adding More Muscle

5

Fast Mass! The "Motionless" Workout

In Part 1, I discussed proper training as the preferred route to optimal muscle development. Proper training, for our purposes, consists of training hard, getting adequate rest, and eating a well-balanced diet. Toward the end of training hard, I've formulated a system of training that I believe is the most effective ever devised.

I've named it the Max Contraction System—M.C.S. for short. As the name implies, it involves firing as many muscle fibers as possible from a position of maximum contraction. This position is not a mere static hold in which the resistance is held randomly at some point in a muscle's range of motion, nor is it a matter of supporting heavy weights statically. Specifically, this system requires a maximal effort to hold the resistance in a position of full muscular contraction for a minimum of forty-five seconds and a maximum of sixty seconds. The goal is to utilize exclusively the anaerobic pathways and not, as in some high-set routines, the aerobic pathways, which can work wonders for improving your endurance but will do precious little in the way of improving your muscle mass.

Remember that intensity and duration exist in an inverse ratio to each other: you can train hard or you can train long, but you can't do both. The unavoidable fact is that it takes hard training—scratch that: it takes *brutally* hard training—to develop massive muscles, and this system is the hardest one in which you will ever engage. Ipso facto, it is the most effective result-producing routine you'll ever use!

Exercise physiologists have defined *intensity* as "increased work per unit of time." In order to increase the work per unit of time, the bodybuilder seeking to grow progressively larger and stronger muscles must make regular attempts to increase the involvement of muscle fibers in a given exercise performed within a given period (that being, in most cases, the duration of a typical set). Doing so causes the body to dip into its muscular reserve ability. Since the body has only a relatively small amount of this reserve on which to draw before a catabolic, or breaking down, effect occurs, it will endeavor to protect itself from future assaults on its highly valued reserves by enlarging on its existing supply of muscle mass. This process, stripped of all the academic and theoretical palaver, is the "secret" to all successful bodybuilding.

It is imperative that you train hard enough to trigger this adaptive response from the body if you want to stimulate compensatory growth. This is where traditional bodybuilding methods have failed the bodybuilder. If you're performing set after set of an arbitrary number of repetitions, you're repeating tasks that are both easy and well within your body's existing ability to handle them. The result? There's absolutely no reason for your body to alter its existing level of muscle mass. No demand, no supply.

To stimulate muscle-mass increases, to really train with an eye toward noticing progress on an almost per-workout basis, you'll have to take each and every set you do for a given body part to the point where 100 percent (or as near to that number as you can come) of a given muscle's fibers have been recruited and stimulated. Intensity of effort is, hands down, the most important factor in increasing both size and strength. Training to what has been labeled "the point of failure," where another second of contraction is impossible despite your greatest effort, ensures that you've passed "the break-over point," which is the point in a set below which growth cannot be stimulated and above which growth will be stimulated.

Once you are able to transcend this break-over point, there will be, as indeed there must be, a marked reduction in the amount of time you can spend training at such a high level of intensity. Therefore, as you're able to adapt to higher and higher levels of intensity, the shorter your workouts must be.

TOWARD A NEW PERSPECTIVE

All right, then. We all understand the nature of adaptation, which is simply a variant of the law of cause and effect. We also understand the supreme importance of intensity of effort. The greater the intensity supplied, the greater the muscular-mass stimulated, and, correspondingly, the briefer the workout must be. What, then, is the method that will allow us to generate *maximum* muscle-fiber involvement and hence *maximum* intensity and, as a result, *maximum* muscle growth?

The answer is a method that focuses on stressing each individual muscle group in the position that involves the maximum amount of muscle fibers for a time span of forty-five to sixty seconds. When using the Max Contraction System, you must throw out all preconceived notions of training methodology. You will no longer be using repetitions to gauge your progress. From now on, you will be counting seconds. You will no longer be looking for a variety of exercises to tax various muscle groups. Instead you will use one exercise only per bodypart that calls into play all of that muscle group's existing muscle fibers—and you will contract that muscle group maximally for the prescribed time until each fiber has been individually spent and you can no longer hold the resistance in the fully contracted ("max") position.

Indeed, this training system is different, but from the time I created it and published the preliminary results of my research back in 1986 until the present day, it has put more muscle mass on more trainees than any other training system I've seen.

THE THEORY

Most of the material on which the Max Contraction System is based is derived from empirically validated data going back more than a hundred years in some instances, and also on common sense, as opposed to commercial interests. What has worked in experiments and physiology labs can be repeated in the gym with equal, if not greater, success. To make it happen, you need to apply yourself diligently to the task at hand, be open-minded enough to be able to throw off the shackles of traditional training "wisdom," and follow the tenets in this chapter. I guarantee that if you do, in the space of a month you will make muscular progress that would otherwise have taken you years to achieve.

It is essential when embarking on a system such as M.C.S. to understand the basic physiological principle of "all or nothing" in regard to muscle-fiber contraction. The principle states, in effect, that when a muscle contracts, a small percentage of its fibers will contract as forcefully as possible, and the rest of its fibers do not contract at all—as opposed to all of the fibers contracting at once but in a lesser degree. A muscle fiber will contract maximally or not at all; this is a bipolar condition that is immutable. With this in mind, it stands to reason that the surest way to involve the most muscle fibers in a given contraction is to engage the muscle group in the portion of the exercise in which all the muscle fibers in that muscle group that can be activated will be activated.

In a normal set of leg extensions, for instance, one starts a given movement from a position of zero resistance, moves into a position of slightly greater resistance, and finally ascends to a position of maximum resistance. This final position, the one in which the most stress is placed on a given muscle group and hence the most muscle-fiber involvement and intensity is generated, is over traditionally almost before it starts. For example, the trainee performing a leg extension will start the movement using only the barest number of muscle fibers required to do the job; at the halfway point, a few more muscle fibers have been activated; and then, at the position of full muscular contraction, as many fibers as possible are activated to hold the resistance in this position. But then, long before the fibers are stressed maximally, the resistance is lowered (often dropped), giving the momentarily stressed quadriceps muscles a chance to disengage and recover—the opposite effect of what we're trying to accomplish. What it boils down to is that, in a given ten-rep set, which lasts about sixty seconds, maximum muscular involvement takes place for a total of only ten seconds—and at that, for only

one second after every five. So, out of a possible sixty seconds' worth of maximum muscular involvement and growth stimulation, the trainee is obtaining only one-tenth of the stimulation that is capable of being generating from the movement. The other nine-tenths of the time devoted to the exercise is essentially wasted.

Conversely, when a given muscle group is made to contract fully against resistance, the most muscle fibers it can activate to assist with the task will be activated and subsequently fatigued, until finally, they are all utilized and spent. At this point, where the resistance can no longer be supported and the contraction must be broken, the resistance is returned slowly to the position of full extension.

As soon as you can no longer hold the contraction, you will have effectively exhausted all the fibers involved in that contraction, which would be all (or at least most) of them. Remember that with M.C.S., you are initiating the "rep" in a position of full muscular contraction. That's what separates this method from other "motionless exercise" systems, such as isometrics, in which contraction is initiated when the fewest number of fibers are activated (i.e., at the beginning of most movements, where a muscle is weakest and the number of fibers involved is minimal, such as the bottom quarter of the press, or arm curls against a doorknob). With such systems, you never progress beyond that minimum level of fiber involvement.

As soon as you can no longer hold the contraction—in this case, with the muscles of the shoulders—you will have effectively stimulated the muscle group you are training into growth.

When you can no longer sustain the contraction, the set is over.

The Max Contraction System utilizes complete and absolute muscular contraction (with added resistance). For advanced trainees, the method of "strip-offs," or Omega Sets™, can be employed. For example, in an exercise such as lat pulldowns, when it becomes impossible to hold your elbows at the level of your lower ribs (the position of full muscular contraction for the lats), and your elbows start to return to the top, weight could be removed, or "stripped off." The benefit is that it enables the trainee to resume another maximum contraction for another forty-five to sixty seconds, until the Max Contraction is broken again—and continuing until even the static holding of a very light weight becomes impossible. This will effectively stimulate every available muscle fiber—and drilling your reserves this deep could well require up to seventy-two hours of rest (perhaps much more) to allow for full recovery and growth

in the form of overcompensation as a result of the workout.

In most cases, maximum growth will be stimulated by the performance of just one Max Contraction set. I supervised the training of a client recently who trained one day a week on a Max Contraction program comprising one forty-five- to sixty-second set of eleven different exercises. This approach totals between eight minutes, fifty-five seconds and eleven minutes per whole-body workout, or between twenty-five and one-half and thirty-three total minutes of training time per week. At the end of five weeks, the subject's strength had improved by a minimum of 100 percent over his starting levels in *all* exercises. More important for our purposes, his lean body-mass increase (i.e., his muscle mass) was a total of sixteen pounds! Try to recall the last time you gained sixteen pounds of pure muscle tissue over a five-week period, and you'll begin to appreciate how effective the Max Contraction System is!

Similar results have been recorded for many other subjects over the twenty years since the system's inception. The lowest muscle-mass increase was eight pounds—and that was on a highly advanced bodybuilder who was already very close to the upper limits of his genetic potential, and who hadn't gained a pound of muscle in more than four years of training on his previous system.

Certainly, you can match this achievement, give or take a few pounds, once you embark on the Max Contraction System. Its stunning success derives from the fundamental principle that anything involving positive and negative resistance has, perforce, fluctuating levels of intensity. As has been established, the closer the resistance is to the fully contracted position (i.e., in a movement in which maximal resistance is truly in a position of full muscular contraction), the more muscle fibers are involved, or activated, by the stressor. In each Max Contraction exercise, all of the fibers are under a constant stress, or intensity, of the highest order from the moment the contraction is initiated until its completion forty-five to sixty seconds later.

THE EXERCISES

To derive the most benefit from M.C.S. training, it is vital to select exercises that allow you to activate the maximum number of a given muscle's fibers while in the fully contracted position. Certain exercises performed with conventional equipment don't incorporate the proper physics to provide resistance in the maximum contraction position. I'm thinking here of movements such as squats, barbell curls (in which the resistance falls off once you pass the halfway point of the movement), and most types of pressing movements. It is this lack of direct resistance in the position of complete muscular contraction that makes these exercises inefficient in an M.C.S. training program.

For M.C.S. training, you must select exercises that enable a targeted muscle group to be contracted completely with maximum resistance for forty-five to sixty seconds. The following list is provided as a guide. It matches major bodyparts with the exercises that have been found to be the best for the purpose of stimulating maximum muscle-fiber involvement and, thus, maximum muscle growth:

1. **Quadriceps:** Leg extensions
2. **Hamstrings:** Leg curls
3. **Calves:** Standing calf raises
4. **Lats:** Lat machine pull-overs, or lat pull-downs (with special Max straps)
5. **Traps:** Shrugs (barbell or dumbbell)
6. **Delts:** Lateral raises (front, side, or rear)
7. **Pectorals:** Pec decks or cable crossovers
8. **Triceps:** Dumbbell kickbacks (or Max straps kickbacks)

9. **Biceps:** Chin-ups (flexed-arm hang) or steep-angle barbell curls
10. **Forearms:** Barbell wrist curls
11. **Abs:** Weighted crunches

The Exercises Explained

1. **Quadriceps: Leg extensions.** Sit at a leg extension machine and place your feet behind the roller pads so that your knees are snug against the seat. Keeping your head and shoulders straight, slowly straighten both legs until you reach the fully contracted position. Sustain this Max Contraction for 45–60 seconds.

2. **Hamstrings: Leg curls.** Lie facedown on the leg curl machine and place your feet under the roller pads, with your knees just over the edge of the bench. Slowly curl your lower legs up until they're almost touching your buttocks. Once in this fully contracted position, sustain this Max Contraction for 45–60 seconds.

3. **Calves: Standing calf raises.** Step underneath the shoulder pads of a standing calf raise machine so that your heels are on the required block and almost touching the ground. From this position of full stretch, slowly contract your calves until you are completely up on your toes. Sustain this Max Contraction for 45–60 seconds.

4. **Lats: Lat machine pull-overs, or lat pull-downs (with special Max straps).** Grab the lat pull-down bar with a palms-under grip, so

Standing calf raise—Max Contraction position.

your arms are fully extended above your head. Slowly contract your lats by pulling the bar down to your chest. Sustain this Max Contraction for 45–60 seconds.

5. **Traps: Shrugs (barbell or dumbbell).** Grab a heavy barbell or a set of dumbbells and straighten your back so that the weight is in front of your thighs. Slowly contract your traps so that your shoulders begin to ascend toward your ears. When the weight has been raised as high as it can go, sustain the Max Contraction for 45–60 seconds.

Lat machine pull-over—Max Contraction position.

Shrug (you can use barbells, dumbbells, or machines)—Max Contraction position.

6. Delts: Lateral raises (forward, side, or bent-over).

Forward raises: Grasp the dumbbells and hold them just in front of your thighs, with your arms perfectly straight. Raise the resistance to the fully contracted position. Sustain this Max Contraction for 45–60 seconds.

Side lateral raises: Hold the dumbbells at your thighs, with your body perfectly erect and your back straight. Smoothly, with lateral head output only and with your elbows locked, begin to raise the dumbbells

Forward raise—Max Contraction position.

Side lateral raise—Max Contraction position.

Bent-over lateral raise—Max Contraction position.

to a height just above shoulder level. Sustain this Max Contraction for 45–60 sconds.

Bent-over laterals: Grasp two dumbbells, one in each hand, and bend over from the waist. Keeping your arms straight, and remaining in the bent-over position, lift the dumbbells toward the ceiling. When the dumbbells have reached the apex of their ascent, sustain this Max Contraction position for 45–60 seconds.

7. Pectorals: Cable crossovers, Pec decks. Adjust the seat until the shoulders (when elbows are together) are directly under the axis of the overhead cams. Fasten the seatbelt (if your machine has one) and place your forearms behind and firmly against the arm pads. Some machines have handles instead of arm pads, in which case simply reach out and take hold of the handles. Try to touch your elbows (or the handles) together in front of your chest. Sustain this Max Contraction position for 45–60 seconds.

Cable crossover—Max Contraction position.

8. Triceps: Dumbbell kickbacks (or Max straps kickbacks). Despite its title, this movement has nothing to do with paying off people who are mentally deficient. It is, rather, an

Steep-angle barbell curl—Max Contraction position.

Barbell wrist curl—Max Contraction position.

exercise that one performs with a dumbbell as opposed to a barbell. To begin, grab hold of a light dumbbell with your right hand and bend forward from the waist, supporting yourself with your free hand. Slowly contract the triceps muscle in your right arm, which will result in the forearm extending beyond the midline of your body. Hold this fully contracted position for 45–60 seconds.

9. Biceps: Steep-angle barbell curl, chin-ups. Grasp the chin-up bar with a palms-up grip. Slowly begin to contract the muscles in your arms, and try to touch the bar to your lower chest when you have reached the apex of your ascent. Hold this contracted position for 45–60 seocnds.

10. Forearms: Barbell wrist curls. Take hold of a barbell in both hands, with your palms facing forward, and sit on the end of a bench. Lift the barbell so that your forearms are resting across the tops of your thighs and the barbell is over the ends of your knees. From this position, slowly curl your wrists upward as far as they can go. Sustain this Max Contraction position for 45–60 seconds.

11. Abs: Crunches. Lie faceup on the floor with your hands behind your head. Try to keep your chin on your chest throughout the movement. Lift your feet up on top of a bench, with your legs slightly apart. From this starting position, slowly curl your

Crunch—Max Contraction position.

trunk upward toward a sitting position. Sustain this Max Contraction position for 45–60 seconds. Add weights for an added workout.

These exercises place a constant stress, or tension, on the target muscle groups from beginning to end. They therefore are the most productive exercises possible owing to their extremely high intensity threshold.

Remember that there are no repetitions involved in this program. Think only in terms of seconds on the clock. In a normal set of ten repetitions, the time frame is typically between forty-five and sixty seconds, but the intensity level varies throughout the range of motion. In M.C.S., one "set" also takes between forty-five and sixty seconds to perform, but the intensity is the highest possible throughout the duration of the set, thus allowing for greater growth stimulation to actually take place.

When commencing any exercise M.C.S. style, lift the resistance slowly, so as not to

damage any ligaments or muscle tissue, up to the position of full muscular contraction, as you would if you were performing a regular set. Then, instead of lowering the weight, hold this fully contracted position for a minimum of forty-five seconds (shoot for sixty seconds) or until the contraction can no longer be held.

If you can hold the resistance for more than sixty seconds, then it's too light, and you should heavy it up by 5 percent by the next workout. If you can't hold the contraction for a full forty-five seconds, then it's too heavy, and you should reduce the resistance by 5 percent until you can contract the muscle for a full forty-five seconds.

You may require a spotter (or two) to lift the weight into the fully contracted position for you. Make sure the spotter doesn't just "drop" the weight off to you, as the sudden shock to the joint of articulation could prove traumatic. Every movement must be done slowly, particularly the settling into the fully contracted position. You may notice your target muscle group begin to shake violently at about the thirty- to forty-second mark, but that's fine. It's an indicator that your muscles are firing up more and more fibers to maintain the contraction, and the more they use, the greater the growth stimulation!

After an M.C.S. workout, you will feel as if your limbs are made of Jell-O, owing to the high volume of activated muscle fibers. To reap maximum growth gains from this system, you must now rest completely, refraining from other forms of strenuous exercise, until your next workout some forty-eight hours later. Structure your workouts forty-eight hours apart, such as Monday, Wednesday, and Friday, with Tuesday, Thursday, Saturday, and Sunday off for recovery and growth.

Eat a proper diet, get adequate rest, and train as hard as you possibly can on this program. You can do two M.C.S. sets of an exercise if you feel so inclined, but remember the intensity/duration inverse continuum and always strive for increased intensity via additional seconds of full contraction. Adhere to these guidelines, and you should realize the best gains of your bodybuilding career!

6

Introducing the Split Routine

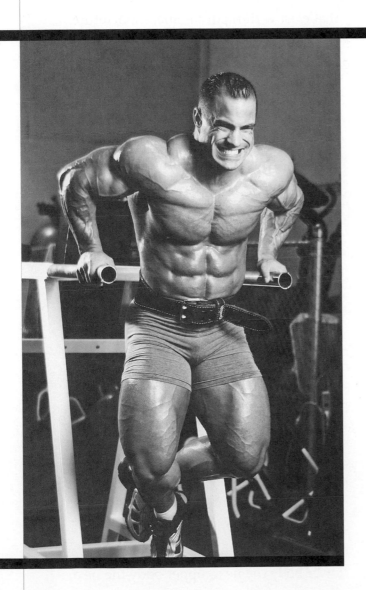

If you've been following along from the beginning, this will now be your fifth month of training. With that in mind, we're going to change our procedure in order to prevent the muscles from becoming too accustomed to the rigors of Max Contraction Training. This chapter also introduces new principles that will broaden your bodybuilding terminology and knowledge, not to mention keep you motivated psychologically, which is perhaps the most important factor in determining your ultimate success in bodybuilding.

As you did last month, you're going to keep your total sets per workout to between ten and twelve, but unlike with all of your previous training, this month you will be using a split routine. In my column in *Ironman* magazine, I've often stated that a workout that stresses the entire body and is performed only one time to three times per week is the most productive way to train—and it happens to be true. However, training on a split routine can be productive if the routine is structured properly.

As a rule, a split routine is not as effective as a whole-body workout in stimulating maximum overall muscle growth. Nevertheless, if you adhere to the major principles of proper exercise—intense, brief, and infrequent workouts—then success will follow, albeit perhaps not as quickly.

After all, virtually every top bodybuilding champion eventually comes to embrace a split-routine approach to training. While other factors enter into the decision to employ this method, the fact remains that lots of muscle has been built by this approach. Even legendary high-intensity advocate Mike Mentzer advocated training on a split routine, and he used it himself in preparing for his runs at the Mr. Olympia title. You would be hard pressed to find a bodybuilder who displayed the massive, dense muscularity of Mentzer when at his peak.

THE RIGHT WAY AND THE WRONG WAY

The secret, if you can call it such, lies in not overtraining or adding more sets to your program while employing the split-routine approach. Doing so would only rob the principles of their value. Don't abuse it, and you'll grow; abuse it, and you'll shrink. (Sounds more like a caveat from a sex therapist than a bodybuilding edict, but anyway . . .)

All right, how does one incorporate this principle of split-routine training? And if it's not as efficacious as a full-body routine, why am I even bothering to tell you about it?

I'll answer the second question first: I'm introducing you to the principle because this book has been designed to educate you, the aspiring bodybuilder, about the myriad methods of training, both good and bad, that exist within our fanatical subculture. Some of these methods work great, such as full-body high-intensity workouts; others don't work at all, such as high-set, multiple split routines conducted over a six- to seven-day period; and some work fairly well, such as high-intensity split routines conducted three times per week. As a serious bodybuilder, you owe it to yourself to understand, or at least be aware of, all of these methods, learn their weaknesses and strengths, and incorporate the positive elements into your own training. Sometimes a properly conducted split routine can provide the necessary change of pace to bring growth back into complacent muscles and also serve to keep your enthusiasm primed and fresh. Once you've passed your plateau, you can always switch back to your full-body routine.

As to how to include the split routine in your training program, I'll start with what *not* to do. A properly conducted split routine doesn't mean training upper body one day, lower body the next, upper body the next, and so on, for an entire week. This would be overtraining from the start and would lead to nothing except reduced progress. Instead, a properly conducted split routine consists of no more than three workouts per week, as in the whole-body routines, spread out with a minimum of forty-eight hours elapsing between workouts to allow for both recovery and growth. Remember that muscle growth is a three-phase process.

A TYPICAL ROUTINE

For your split routine, you will train three bodyparts on Monday, train three alternate body parts on Wednesday, and then repeat Monday's workout on Friday. For example:

- **Monday:** Legs, chest, and biceps
- **Wednesday:** Back, shoulders, and triceps
- **Friday:** Legs, chest, and biceps
- **Monday of the following week:** Back, shoulders, and triceps

This structure will help ensure that all muscle groups are thoroughly stimulated but not overtrained. Your total sets per bodypart will also be low (a maximum of four) in order to provide a higher intensity level in your workouts. If too many sets are performed, you will find yourself fighting a natural inclination to "hold back" something for the succeeding set. Every set should be taken to muscular failure, in which an additional repetition is impossible despite your greatest effort.

The bodyparts to be trained in each workout are structured the way I've listed them for a reason. Recall that a highly trained muscle needs a minimum of forty-eight hours to recover and grow from a workout. In fact, 2006 research (Nautilus North Study 2006; *Advanced Max Contraction Training*, McGraw-Hill, 2006) indicates that one week is required for the body to fully recover and grow. In some cases, when you've really been able to drill deep, you may need upward of two weeks to both recover and grow from a workout. However, these frequency issues apply more to intermediate and advanced trainees than beginners. For now, we'll stay with the three-days-per-week workout—only this time employing a split routine.

Reading this, you may be alarmed to realize that on this program some bodyparts will be trained only once a week and that, consequently, a period of 168 hours will pass before they are trained again. That time structure takes you beyond what some physiologists believe to be the dangerous "ninety-six-hour" mark; i.e., that a highly trained muscle must be trained again within ninety-six hours or else it will reduce size and strength. (This belief has been shown to be in serious error, however, particularly as it applies to newcomers to bodybuilding who are not yet capable of generating the type of intensity in their workouts that requires upward of a week off between workouts, and so the ninety-six-hour mark is a good benchmark for the outer limits of training frequency at the beginner's stage.)

Following the ninety-six-hour-mark rule for the time being, a split routine can work well within these confines provided you have selected your exercises carefully. Here, the exercises in your midweek workout also activate, in some capacity, the muscles that you work in your sessions that bookend the week.

For example, on Monday, you will be training legs, chest, and biceps. You know that on Wednesday, any form of shoulder press, chinning motion, or triceps extension will involve your chest to some degree and provide maintenance stimulation that will offset the potential for decompensation, or atrophy. Likewise, if you include an exercise such as stiff-legged dead lifts in your back routine, your legs will also benefit from the performance. This should hold for all bodyparts that you train, and the effect is somewhat akin to performing a whole-body routine every workout (alas, my prejudices have crept back in)—the true secret of successful split-routine training!

In short, your leg training contains some back work, your chest training contains some triceps work, and your biceps training contains some shoulder work; your back training contains some leg work and biceps work, and your shoulder routine contains some chest work, as does your triceps training. As you can see, while it's sufficiently diverse to justify being called a split routine, an argument can be made on technical grounds for calling it a whole-body workout.

Speaking of which, let's get on with this month's routine. Since I've covered proper exercise performance in previous chapters,

I won't reiterate protocols with which you're already familiar.

Legs, Chest, and Biceps

1. **Barbell squats:**
   4 × 10–15 reps

2. **Bench presses:**
   2 × 10–12 reps

3. **Dumbbell flyes:**
   2 × 10–12 reps

4. **Barbell curls:**
   2 × 10–20 reps

5. **Alternate dumbbell curls:**
   2 × 10–12 reps

6. **Crunches:**
   1 × 30 reps (optional)

Back, Shoulders, and Biceps

1. **Stiff-legged dead lifts:**
   2 × 12–15 reps

2. **Barbell shrugs:**
   2 × 10–12 reps

3. **Bent-over barbell rows:**
   2 × 10–15 reps

4. **Lat pull-downs:**
   2 × 10–12 reps

5. Lying triceps extensions:
2 × 10–12 reps

6. Standing French presses:
2 × 10–12 reps

Routine One Explained: Legs, Chest, and Biceps

1. Barbell squats: Stand erect with a barbell across your shoulders and take a deep breath. With your lungs full, bend your knees and lower your body until you are in a full squat position; you should be slightly below a ninety-degree angle to your shins. As soon as you reach the bottom position, rise immediately—but under control—while at the same time expelling the air from your lungs, so that you will be ready for another intake of oxygen at the completion of the movement. Breathe in, and go down for a second repetition until you have completed your set. It is important to keep your head up at all times, and your chest should be held high.

2. Bench presses: Lie on a bench with a barbell at arm's length over your chest. Slowly lower the bar to your upper chest. Once the bar has touched your chest, slowly press it back up to the top position, and repeat the procedure for the required number of sets and repetitions.

3. Dumbbell flyes: Grab two fairly heavy dumbbells and lie faceup on a bench. Slowly lower the dumbbells from an overhead position in an outward arc until they are a bit below chest level. Pause for one or two

seconds, and then begin to slowly raise the dumbbells back to the starting overhead position in the same outward arc.

4. Standing barbell curls: Stand erect with a shoulder-width grip on the barbell and your palms facing front. Your arms should be fully extended so that the barbell is directly in front of your thighs. Slowly curl the barbell up to shoulder height, solely using the muscles of the upper arm by bending the elbows. From this fully contracted position, slowly lower the resistance back to the fully extended (or starting) position. Repeat for the required number of sets and repetitions.

5. Alternate dumbbell curls: Take hold of two dumbbells and stand up straight with dumbbells at your sides and your palms facing your hips. Slowly curl your right arm up to your right shoulder, making sure to turn your palm upward at the top of the movement. As your right arm is starting to come down, start curling your left arm upward, making sure that one arm is descending while the other is ascending. Repeat until you have completed 10–12 repetitions per arm.

6. Crunches: Lie faceup on the floor with your hands behind your head. Keep your chin on your chest throughout the movement. Lift your feet up on top of a bench, with your feet together and your knees facing left and right. Slowly curl your trunk upward toward a sitting position. Once you have ascended to a fully contracted position, hold the position for a two-count, and then lower yourself slowly back to the starting position. Repeat for the required number of repetitions.

Routine Two Explained: Back, Shoulders, and Biceps

1. Stiff-legged dead lifts: Stand erect with your feet just under the barbell. Then, by bending your knees, grasp the barbell, with your hands a little wider apart than shoulder width and your knuckles facing front. Slowly begin to stand erect, straightening your legs as you do so. Keep lifting the resistance until you're completely erect and the bar is in front of your thighs. Now slowly lower the resistance until it is back on the floor, and repeat the movement for the required number of sets and repetitions. Rest briefly, and then move on to your next exercise.

2. Barbell shrugs: Grab a heavy barbell and straighten your back so that the weight is in front of your thighs. Slowly contract your traps so that your shoulders begin to ascend toward your ears. When the weight has been raised as high as it can go, hold the contraction for a two-count, and then lower the weight slowly, in four seconds, back to the starting position.

3. Bent-over barbell rows: Bend at the waist so that your torso is at a right angle (ninety degrees) to your legs. Grab hold of the bar so that your palms are facing

your shins. Your hand spacing should be between two and two and a half feet. Slowly pull the bar up toward your torso until it touches your lower chest. From this fully contracted position, slowly lower the resistance back to the starting position (your arms should be fully extended), and repeat for the required number of sets and repetitions. Remember that the barbell is to touch the floor only when the set is completed. This will ensure that maximum stimulation is imparted to the lats throughout the movement. Also remember to maintain the bent-over position throughout the set.

4. Lat pull-downs: Grab the lat pull-down bar with a palms-under grip, so your arms are fully extended above your head. Slowly contract your lats by pulling the bar down to your chest. Hold this position of full muscular contraction for a two-count before allowing the weight to return in four seconds back to the starting position.

5. Lying triceps extensions: Lie on an exercise bench, holding a barbell (or E-Z curl bar) in both hands directly over your chest. Slowly lower the resistance, in four seconds, to a point just behind your head. From this fully extended position, slowly press the resistance back up to the starting position. Use your first set as a slow, controlled, warm-up set, and then add approximately 20 percent more to the bar and perform another set of 10–12 repetitions.

6. Standing French presses: Grab an E-Z curl bar and press it overhead. Then, instead of lowering your elbows, keep them stationary and just lower your forearms. The bar should be lowered to a point just below the back of your neck in four seconds, and, with no momentum whatsoever, your triceps should slowly power the bar back to the arms-locked starting position.

Always strive to add another repetition to your previous best attempt in this exercise. Once the guide number of repetitions has been reached, increase the resistance that you have been using by 5 percent, and aim for the lower guide number of reps again.

Maintain perfect form while working out under this or any other training system. A loosening of form results in less stress being placed on the target muscle group and will greatly diminish your results. Lift the resistance slowly in two to three seconds; hold it for one to two seconds at the top, or fully contracted position; and then lower it slowly, in four seconds, back to the starting position.

This routine is a highly effective one if executed along the guidelines given. Give it a try, and you should notice a distinct increase in your muscle mass over the next four weeks.

7

Giant Sets

In Chapter 6 we experimented with a split routine and found, or should have found, that it does yield certain benefits in terms of muscular growth. In order to keep your muscles growing, however, you must continue to provide the necessary stimulus. In other words, you're going to have to provide your central nervous system with a reason for altering your body's existing muscular condition. This can be accomplished only by upping the intensity of your workouts—by doing something more demanding than what your body is accustomed to performing during your regular training sessions.

In fact, your "regular" training session is going to have to become highly "irregular" in order for this adaptive response to occur. This, in turn, can be accomplished in any of a number of ways: by pushing past the traditional "failure" point in a set via forced reps, negatives, and/or descending sets;

by altering your workload via performing more sets in less time (for example, by using supersets, tri-sets, and giant sets—as explained in the following section); by specializing on a different bodypart; or by changing either the exercises or the order in which they're traditionally performed within your routine.

Any of these methods will assure you of perpetually placing an order for muscular change with your central nervous system. This is also referred to in the bodybuilding vernacular as "confusing" or "shocking" the muscles, although the muscles themselves have no powers of cognition; they simply contract and relax and are impervious to any form of befuddlement.

BEYOND SUPERSETS

This brings us to the introduction of giant sets and tri-sets to both your bodybuilding lexicon and training routine. First off, I can assure you that giant sets involve nothing Brobdingnagian. Giant sets are simply supersets with four to six exercises that are performed in rapid-fire succession (without any rest in between), one set of each at a time, to make for one extended—or "giant"—set. The same is true of tri-sets except, as the term implies, only three exercises are involved. (Tradition has revealed that any number over three constitutes "giant" in a bodybuilder's mind.)

Both methods involve the use of several different exercises that all tax the same bodypart. For example, in training the biceps in giant set fashion, you would choose four biceps exercises, such as preacher (or Scott) curls with a barbell (detailed in Chapter 8), standing barbell curls, incline dumbbell curls, and standing dumbbell curls. You would perform your first set of preacher curls for, say, twelve reps, and as soon as you complete this set, you would immediately pick up a preloaded barbell and perform your second biceps exercise—standing barbell curls—again, for twelve reps (to the point of failure), and as soon as you finish this exercise, you would immediately advance to the next exercise—incline dumbbell curls—for another set of twelve reps, and from here, you would go to your final biceps exercise—standing dumbbell curls—and knock off a final set of twelve reps to complete your first giant set.

"Did you say *first*?" (I can hear your silent query.) That's correct. A giant set is the equivalent of performing one (very) extended set. Granted, it is highly draining and demanding. In fact, one giant set is often sufficient stimulation for a muscle group. Nevertheless, it is still just your *first* set. As I've mentioned before, when it comes to specialization, you're generally allowed a maximum of five sets per bodypart without running the risk of overtraining. Now, I'm not recommending that you do five giant sets composed of four exercises per bodypart, although champions such as Robby Robinson have done so effectively. Without their years of training background and their genetic capacity to tolerate such workouts, it would be akin to rolling out of bed, with no training, and heading off to compete in your first triathlon! You must build up your conditioning to such exercise before attempting such a dramatic increase in training volume.

If you want to experience muscle growth as opposed to a catabolic, or muscle-destroying, state, you are well advised to keep your total number of giant sets to the absolute minimum required to get the job done. The same advice applies to your overall number of standard workout sets, for that matter. It must also be noted that the majority of top bodybuilders who perform such high-volume workouts successfully have more than a passing acquaintance with anabolic steroids, which act as a catalyst in the recovery and anabolic (tissue building) processes.

A giant set, again, is tantamount to an extended set. To continue with our biceps example, if you should hit failure on your first set of preacher curls at twelve reps, the remaining sets would then become a form of self-generated forced reps, which enable you to keep contracting your biceps muscles under the stress of an imposed workload for a period beyond what you would be able to manage otherwise. It's not unlike receiving thirty-six forced reps after hitting failure on your first set of preacher curls. But enough similes, let's get down to the actual training!

This routine is going to have you train, again, three days per week (Monday,

Wednesday, and Friday) so that in any workout you're not training more than two bodyparts utilizing giant sets. Doing too much of this particular training method will invariably prove too taxing for your central nervous system to produce any results whatever. On Monday, you will train your legs and shoulders (Workout One); on Wednesday, you will be training your chest and triceps (Workout Two); and on Friday, you'll be training your back and biceps (Workout Three). You'll rest over the weekend and then start the cycle over again on the following Monday.

Here is the workout routine:

WORKOUT ONE

Legs and Shoulders

LEGS

1. Calf raises:
20 reps

2. Leg curls:
15 reps

3. Leg extensions:
15 reps

4. Squats:
15 reps

Perform four giant sets of the preceding four movements, rest for two to three minutes, and then move on to your second body part—shoulders!

SHOULDERS

1. Seated/standing dumbbell laterals:
12 reps

2. Seated dumbbell presses:
12 reps

3. Bent-over laterals:
12 reps

4. Seated dumbbell shrugs:
12 reps

Again, repeat the four exercises without rest until you have completed your first giant set; then rest briefly for one to two minutes before hitting it again three more times.

WORKOUT TWO

Chest and Triceps

CHEST

1. Incline dumbbell presses:
10 reps

2. Dumbbell flyes:
12 reps

3. Bench presses:
12 reps

Perform four tri-sets of these three exercises, and your chest should be swollen up like a zeppelin! Also remember to perform all of your reps slowly and smoothly, with no sudden jerks or thrusts. This isn't Olympic lifting; this is bodybuilding, which means you must make a concerted effort to ensure that it's your muscles, and not momentum, doing all of the work during this exercise. After a short break, it's time to train your triceps, so get ready, because this is one killer routine that will pump your arms up at least a solid inch!

TRICEPS

1. Seated French presses:
12 reps

2. Cable push-downs:
12 reps

3. Lying triceps extensions:
12 reps

Perform four tri-sets of the preceding three movements, making sure that you get all twelve reps. Don't compromise exercise form in order to make the rep count, and don't stop short of the prescribed number of reps; hit the full twelve, and then move on to the next set until four tri-sets have been completed.

WORKOUT THREE

Back and Biceps

BACK

1. Dumbbell pull-overs:
12 reps

2. Close-grip pull-downs:

12 reps

3. Barbell rows:

12 reps

You'll really find yourself breathing quickly after your second exercise in this tri-set cycle, but push yourself through one more set before you take a one- to two-minute breather in between tri-sets. Then repeat the cycle for three more tri-sets before moving on to everybody's favorite muscle group—the biceps!

BICEPS

1. Dumbbell curls:

12 reps

2. Barbell curls:

12 reps

3. Preacher curls:

12 reps

4. Reverse-grip preacher curls:

12 reps

Perform three sets of the preceding four exercises, and your biceps will look and feel like fully inflated basketballs! This giant set will hit your biceps like nothing ever has before—and will you be glad that the next two days are "rest days"! Anyone who completes a three-day split routine of tri-sets and giant sets certainly deserves at least a

couple of days off before hitting that sort of routine again. When training with giant sets, always move quickly from exercise to exercise until you've completed all three or four in a row without any rest. At this point, you can rest briefly before repeating the giant set. In all, perform each giant set four times unless otherwise noted.

Workout One Explained

LEGS

1. Calf raises: Step underneath the shoulder pads of a standing calf raise machine so that your heels are on the required block and almost touching the ground. From this position of full stretch, slowly contract your calves until you are completely up on your toes. Hold this position for a two-count before lowering yourself in four seconds back to the starting position.

2. Leg curls: Lie facedown on the leg curl machine and place your feet under the roller pads, with your knees just over the edge of the bench. Slowly curl your lower legs up until they're almost touching your buttocks. Once in this fully contracted position, hold the contraction for a two-count, and then lower the resistance slowly back to the starting position.

3. Leg extensions: Sit at a leg extension machine and place your feet behind the roller pads so that your knees are snug against

Calf raise—Start position.

Calf raise—Finish position.

the seat. Keeping your head and shoulders straight, slowly straighten both legs until you reach the fully contracted position. Pause briefly, and then lower under control.

4. **Barbell squats:** Stand erect with a barbell across your shoulders and take a deep breath. With your lungs full, bend your knees and lower your body until you are in a full squat position. You should be slightly below a ninety-degree angle to your shins. As soon as you reach the bottom position, rise immediately—but under control—while at the same time expelling the air from your lungs so that you will be ready for an intake

of breath at the completion of the movement. Breathe in and go down for a second squat and repeat until you have completed the required number of repetitions. See Chapter 1 for a full description of this exercise.

SHOULDERS

1. **Seated/standing dumbbell laterals:** This is a terrific isolation movement for the lateral head of the deltoid; in addition, it heavily activates the trapezius muscle during the last quarter of the movement. From a standing position, grab two dumbbells and hold them

Standing dumbbell lateral—Start position.

Standing dumbbell lateral—Finish position.

at your sides, with your palms facing each other. Keeping your arms straight and using only your shoulder muscles, slowly lift the weight up to, and a bit higher than, shoulder level. Hold this position of full contraction for a two-count before lowering the dumbbells slowly, in four seconds, back to the starting position.

2. Seated dumbbell presses: This exercise works the deltoids, particularly the medial deltoid, and the upper trapezius, serratus anterior, and triceps. Sit down on a bench so that your back is straight. Grasp two dumbbells wtih your palms facing forward and lift them to your shoulders. Press your arms up overhead until they are fully locked out. Pause briefly in this position and then

lower the dumbbells back to your shoulders. Repeat for the required number of repetitions.

3. Bent-over laterals: Grasp light dumbbells, one in each hand, and bend over from the waist. Keeping your arms straight, and remaining in the bent-over position, lift the dumbbells toward the ceiling. When the dumbbells have reached the apex of their ascent, really tighten up that rear deltoid head and then lower the dumbbells, slowly, to the count of four seconds.

4. Seated dumbbell shrugs: Take hold of a pair of dumbbells and sit down on a flat bench. Keeping your arms extended and your palms facing toward each other, slowly

Seated dumbbell press—Start position.

Seated dumbbell press—Finish position.

Bent-over lateral—Start position.

Bent-over lateral—Finish position.

shrug your shoulders up as lightly as you can. Pause briefly at the top (in a fully contracted position) and then slowly lower your arms back down to where they were. Repeat for 12 repetitions.

Workout Two Explained

CHEST

1. Incline dumbbell presses: This exercise works the pectorals very strongly, along with the anterior deltoids, serratus anterior, and pectoralis minor (the latter two serve to stabilize the scapulae), and the triceps. Lie back on an incline bench with your elbows bent. Hold the dumbbells with your palms facing forward. Extend your arms until they

Seated dumbbell shrug—Finish position.

Incline dumbbell press—Start position.

Incline dumbbell press—Finish position.

Dumbbell fly   Start position.

Dumbbell fly—Finish position

are straight above your head. Pause briefly and then lower the dumbbells back to your shoulders. Repeat for the required number of repetitions.

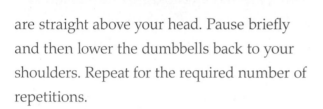

2. **Dumbbell flyes:** Grab two fairly heavy dumbbells and lie faceup on a bench. Slowly lower the dumbbells from an overhead position in an outward arc until they are a bit below chest level. Pause for one or two seconds, and then begin to slowly raise the dumbbells back to the starting overhead position in the same outward arc.

3. **Bench presses:** Lie on a bench with a barbell at arm's length over your chest. Slowly lower the bar to your upper chest. Once the bar has touched your chest (I said "touched," not "bounced"; bouncing a weight accomplishes nothing but injury), slowly press it back up to the top position, and repeat the procedure for the required number of repetitions. Put the weight down,

rest briefly, and then perform your next exercise.

TRICEPS

1. **Seated French presses:** Grab hold of a Triceps Blaster or an E-Z curl bar. Press the weight overhead as if you were about to perform the press behind the neck. Keep your elbows stationary beside your ears and lower your forearms until they are as far down toward the center of your back as they can go. The time structure is the same with this exercise: two seconds up and four seconds down. Repeat for at least eight repetitions. A second set is, again, recommended for beginners and intermediates, but it's not necessary for advanced trainees.

2. **Cable push-downs:** Grasp the bar with a palms-over grip. Your elbows should be planted firmly on the sides of your rib cage. Smoothly extend your arms until

Cable push-down—Start position.

Cable push-down—Finish position.

your elbows are completely locked out. It is important to hold this position of full muscular contraction and to be cognizant of how it feels; this is the only point in the exercise when all three heads of the triceps are contracted fully. After holding this position for a two-count, lower the resistance slowly back to the starting position.

3. **Lying triceps extensions:** Lie on an exercise bench, holding a barbell (or E-Z curl bar) in both hands directly over your chest. From this position, slowly lower the resistance, in four seconds, to a point just behind your head. From this fully extended position, slowly press the resistance back up to the starting position. Just as in the preceding exercise, use your first set as a slow, controlled, warm-up set, and then add approximately 20 percent more to the bar and perform two more sets of 10 repetitions.

Workout Three Explained

BACK

1. **Dumbbell pull-overs:** Grasp a moderately weighted dumbbell in both hands and lie back on a flat bench crosswise so that only your shoulders are touching the bench. Extend the dumbbell beyond your head so that it is almost touching the floor. From this position of full stretch, and with a slight bend in your arms, slowly, with your lats as prime mover, pull the dumbbell over

Close-grip pull-down—Start position.

Close-grip pull-down—Finish position.

your head to approximately your sternum. A deliberate pause in this position should precede your lowering the dumbbell back to the starting position in four seconds.

2. **Close-grip pull-downs:** Place your hands about six inches apart on the bar and pull the bar down to your chest as you sit down. Keep your elbows pointed out to your sides. You may need some counterresistance to be applied to your legs to anchor you when the weights start getting heavy. Hold the fully contracted position for a two-count before returning the resistance to the starting position in four seconds. Repeat for your I.S.R., and have your partner force out three more reps.

3. **Upright barbell rows:** Place your hands about six inches apart on a barbell with an overhand grip (your palms should be facing your thighs). Keeping your body straight and stationary, slowly pull the weight up to your clavicles (collar bone). Keep the barbell in close, and then slowly, in four seconds, lower it back to the starting position.

BICEPS

1. **Dumbbell curls:** Grab a pair of dumbbells and hold them at your sides with the palms touching your upper thighs. Slowly curl both arms up until the dumbbells are at shoulder level. Pause briefly in this fully

Dumbbell curl—Start position.

Dumbbell curl—Finish position.

contracted position, and then lower the dumbbells slowly, in four seconds, back to the starting position. Perform your first set as a slow, controlled, warm-up set, and then increase the resistance by 20 percent (give or take a couple of pounds, depending on your existing strength levels) and superset your next two sets for 10 repetitions each.

2. Standing barbell curls: Stand erect with a shoulder-width grip on the barbell and your palms facing front. Your arms should be fully extended so that the barbell is directly in front of your thighs. Now slowly lift, or curl, the barbell up to shoulder height, solely using the muscles of the upper arm by bending the elbows. From this fully contracted position, slowly lower the resistance back to the fully extended (or starting)

Barbell curl—Start position.

Barbell curl—Finish position.

Preacher curl—Start position.

Preacher curl—Finish position.

position. Repeat for the required number of repetitions, and then rest briefly before performing your next exercise.

3. Preacher curls: The bench used for this exercise should have a steep incline, to ensure resistance in the position of full muscular contraction. Grasp the bar with a shoulder-width grip. Starting from the position of full extension, slowly (in two seconds) raise the bar to throat level, being sure to hold the completely contracted position for a two-count before lowering the bar in four seconds. Repeat the procedure for at least eight repetitions.

4. Reverse-grip preacher curls: The reverse-grip preacher curls require that your grip be the opposite from how you perform preacher curls. You grasp the bar using palm-down

Reverse-grip preacher curl—Finish position.

grip placement with your hands closer than shoulder width apart to work the brachiais muscle of the upper arm. Otherwise, perform the exercise in the exact same way indicated for the preacher curls.

REPETITIONS REVISITED

At this junction, I offer some tips on how to make the foregoing exercises more effective. They're minor variations to be sure, but important enough that if they're not adhered to, you will not derive the maximum results from the exercises and will severely compromise their efficacy.

First, when you execute your repetitions, be focused from full extension to full contraction. Don't just throw the weight up and let it fall back to the starting position of its own accord. Slowly, deliberately, raise the resistance by contracting your target muscle group completely; you'll feel the pain of the lactic acid setting in. If the weight's heavy enough, you should be almost spent at rep number eight, but persevere until you've muscled out twelve of them; that way, your muscles will be sure to be thoroughly stimulated.

If you find that you're breathing too hard, don't push yourself through the exercises merely to "beat the clock." Instead, rest briefly, no more than fifteen seconds, until your breathing returns to normal, and then continue on in your giant set in order to ensure that your muscles, rather than

your cardiovascular system, will receive maximum stimulation.

You will find that this is an especially effective routine for burning calories and developing muscle fast. You definitely won't need to perform any aerobics while you're on this program. You'll be burning more calories from your workouts than you would from running or cycling while at the same time stimulating far-and-away more muscle growth. These routines work, but only if the principles of high-intensity training are followed, such as keeping the workouts brief (no more than thirty to forty-five minutes per session) and infrequent (each bodypart trained only once or twice a week).

It may appear to be more sets than you're accustomed to doing, and if these were "straight sets," you would easily become overtrained on such a program and not progress at all. However, the nature of giant setting and tri-setting is such that doing these one-after-the-other exercises for a selected bodypart is like performing one extended set. Therefore, you're performing only three to four total sets per any given bodypart. This explanation of twelve sets being four sets is probably coming off a little bit like trying to explain the "oneness" of the Trinity of Christianity, but I think if you reread the explanations on why this is so, you'll comprehend my pitch.

Training for Size and Power

The other day I was thumbing through a few of my old muscle magazines and had to laugh out loud at some of the absurd titles of the articles: "I Cried for My Pecs"—Is that how he finally solved his pectoral problem? If so, then I'm off for a very productive weep!; "No-Frills Calf Workout"—Ever heard of a "Frills Calf Workout"?; "Hercules Reincarnated"—I beg your pardon?; "Herculean Back Routine"—Hercules, as you can see, is a popular myth among bodybuilding journalists. Further back I found one entitled "Inside Mohamed Makkaway"—Written by his proctologist perhaps? Then there was "Tim Belknap Says, 'Thanks, Joe!'"—This is newsworthy stuff? What's he going to say next month, "Pass the salt"? One last example: "Bombing for Arm Balance"—Can "Rocket Launching for Symmetry" be far behind?

8

All of these and other so-called articles promised the moon in terms of muscle growth, but upon closer inspection not one of them explained *why* or *how* the touted methods would actually deliver on the promises. There was plenty of rhetoric and advertising boldly proclaiming the "secret" to muscular massiveness. To any student of kinesiology or physiology, the claims were ludicrous; to any layperson wanting to know the best way to train, the claims were downright dangerous.

ACTING ON INSTINCT

It seems at times that bodybuilding has forsaken truth for mysticism: if you take this "magic" supplement or perform this "magic" exercise, everything will come your way. These views no doubt persist due, in large part, to mankind's inherent desire to take the easy way out. Given a choice, most people will take the route of least resistance. They do this primarily out of instinct. As our ancestors likely discovered, the more energy people could conserve while still obtaining the desired results, the more energy would be left for other important activities relevant to survival.

Modern man is no different. Let's say a prospective trainee is told by one individual that his objective of increasing his muscle mass and strength can be accomplished only through brutally hard training, which, while being of necessity brief and infrequent, is nevertheless capable of inducing feelings of nausea,

deep fatigue, and momentary muscle debilitation. Then the initiate is told by another individual that he can obtain the same results simply by increasing his supplementation or by performing several "magical" pumping/flushing, high-volume, triple-split, up-and-down-the-rack, zip-zop, blitz-bomb routines that in no way tax the central nervous system (which is why these routines do not work, incidentally). In fact, the second chap likens these "magic" routines to the experience of "orgasm." Don't laugh: this was a popular belief promulgated by no less than Arnold Schwarzenegger back in the mid- to late 1970s. Now, which do you think any clear-thinking human being would choose? If you guessed the brutally hard routine, you are out of your mind!

The "pleasure-filled" routine is indubitably the more appealing of the two. Unfortunately, it contains no basis of truth and can deliver no results. Even the simile is incongruous: the last thing in the world to which a growth-inducing, heavy set of twenty-rep squats is akin is the feeling of orgasm! Whereas the former is downright hard work, the latter is, well, a jolly good time. The only way such a simile could be accurately invoked is if the one who postulated the comparison were inclined toward masochism.

Leaving the realm of mysticism, we shall now concern ourselves with reality. After six months of development and experimentation, you need a baseline workout to which you can return as a beginner, before moving on to the more advanced material outlined in Part 3. You want a routine that will serve you, as it stands, as an efficient, result-producing base from which you can deviate from time to time for the purpose of specialization. What follows, then, divested of nonessentials, is that routine:

THE ROUTINE

1. Barbell squats:
   2 sets of 15–20 reps

2. Chin-ups:
   2 sets of 8–12 reps

3. Bench presses:
   2 sets of 8–12 reps

4. Seated presses behind the neck:
   2 sets of 8–12 reps

5. Preacher curls:
   1–2 sets of 8–12 reps

6. Seated French presses:
   1–2 sets of 8–12 reps

The Four Pillars of Hypertrophy

If your goal is increased size and strength, then it is important to keep the following four points in mind:

1. The best routine is one that produces results (muscle growth and strength).
2. Muscle growth and strength are obtained through *supply and demand*.
3. The greater the demand on the muscles, the quicker the adaptive response from

the central nervous system to supply that demand (provided adequate rest and nutrition are also supplied).

4. The greater the intensity of your training:
   - The greater the demand on the muscles.
   - The shorter the workout.
   - The greater the need for rest and recovery (forty-eight to ninety-six hours, minimum).

The Routine Explained

1. Barbell squats: No fewer than fifteen muscle groups are involved whenever you perform squats, which unquestionably rates this exercise at the pinnacle of the muscle-building chart. To perform the squat properly, stand erect with a barbell across your shoulders and take a deep breath. With full lungs, bend your knees and lower your body until you are in a full squat position; you should be slightly below a ninety-degree angle to your shins. As soon as you reach the bottom position, rise immediately—but under control—while at the same time exhaling, so that you will be ready for a breath at the completion of the movement. Breathe in and go down for a second repetition and so on until you have completed your set. Remember to keep your head up at all times, and hold your chest up high.

2. Chin-ups: Grasp the chin-up bar with a palms-up grip. (You may require straps to reinforce your grip for the required number of repetitions.) Slowly begin to contract the muscles in your arms, and try to touch the bar to your lower chest when you have reached the apex of your ascent. Hold this contracted position for a two-count, and then lower yourself slowly (four seconds) back to the starting position, all the while making sure that the latissimus dorsi muscles are constantly contracted. Repeat this procedure until at least eight repetitions have been completed. Rest for one to two minutes, and repeat for another eight-to-twelve repetitions.

If you can't perform a chin-up on your own, you may use an assisted chin-up machine: Stand on a chair facing the chin-up bar, grab the bar, and step off. Under full muscle control, lower yourself to a stretched position as slowly as you can. Repeat to exhaustion. When you can complete ten negatives, you should be able to perform at least three or four regular chin-ups.

3. **Bench presses:** Every third week or so, perform this exercise, as described in Chapter 1, first in your routine in order to test your upper-body progress. When testing for strength, as opposed to building it, perform your first set for only five repetitions, rest briefly, and then perform one rep maximum lifts or "singles" with a one-to two-minute rest in between, until you eventually hit a weight that you cannot lift (no more than five sets of singles). Obviously, a training partner is a necessity for maximum single attempts. However, when training for muscle mass and power,

Seated press behind the neck.

perform no more than two sets of eight to twelve repetitions.

4. **Seated presses behind the neck:** Begin with a light poundage in order to warm up your entire shoulder girdle. Take a deep breath before pressing the weight up smoothly to the fully extended position of your arms, and then lower the resistance twice as slowly (four seconds) back to the starting position. Add weight to the bar (approximately 20 percent more than your warm-up weight) and perform one more set.

5. **Preacher curls:** The bench used for this exercise should have a steep incline, to ensure resistance in the position of full muscular contraction. Grasp the bar with a shoulder-width grip. Starting from the position of full extension, slowly (in two seconds) raise the bar to throat level, being sure to hold the completely contracted position for a two-count before lowering the bar in four seconds. Repeat the procedure for at least eight repetitions.

I mentioned earlier that Hercules is a frequently cited figure among bodybuilding scribes, and I am no exception. It has been said that there is a seed of truth in all mythologies, and with that underlying thought, I'd like to share the following story with you.

One day when Hercules was a young man, as he was struggling to decide what direction to take in life, he saw two women approaching him. One of them ran in front to get to him first. She was tall and beautiful and decked out in bright clothing, with her cheeks rather too red to be natural.

She said to him, "Young man, I see you are in doubt about what to do in life and what path to follow, so I invite you to follow me. You shall have the easiest and most pleasant life in the world, with no hard work and no dangers. You shall eat, drink, and be merry. Others shall work, but you shall have the enjoyment, and you shall be as happy as the day is long."

Hercules asked, "What is your name?"

The woman answered, "My real name is Pleasure, but my enemies call me Vice."

By this time, the second woman had caught up to them. She was also tall and handsome but after a different fashion; she was stately and dignified and had a noble look. Her dress was all white, truth was in her eyes, and modesty was in her manner.

She said, "Young sir, I know your parents and your breeding, and how you have been educated and brought up, which makes me hope that you will be a good workman of noble deeds. I will not deceive you with promises of pleasant things; I will tell you the truth: nothing that is really good can be got without labor and hardship, for so the gods have ordained. If you wish to enjoy the fruits of this earth, you must plough and sow, and reap and mow. *So, if you wish your body to be strong, you must make your body the servant to your mind, and fear not labor and sweat.* In the same way, if you wish for the love of friends, you must do good to your friends; if you wish for honor from our city or your native land, you must work for their benefit, and you must defend them from enemies without and tyrants within. If you choose to follow me, I can make you great and truly happy."

Hercules asked, "And what is your name?"

She answered, "My name is Virtue."

Then Pleasure piped up: "See, Hercules, what a hard road she puts before you! Not a scrap of pleasure in it!"

But Virtue said, "Such pleasure as she is offering you leads only to surfeit and weariness. He who tries to be happy never succeeds, but he who does noble deeds gains happiness without trying."

The legend has it that Hercules resolved to follow the hard road and to put away from his mind the craving for pleasure.

And so, in your training, as in your life, do not be duped by those promising pleasure or the easy way out. As Virtue said to Hercules, "Nothing that is really good can be got without labor and hardship." This is especially true in bodybuilding; there is no such thing as "magic" in stimulating muscle growth—only "labor and sweat."

6. **Seated French presses:** Grab a Triceps Blaster or an E-Z curl bar. Press the weight overhead as if you were about to perform the press behind the neck. Keep your elbows stationary beside your ears and lower your forearms until they are as far down toward the center of your back as they can go. The time structure is the same with this exercise: two seconds up and four seconds down. Repeat for at least eight repetitions.

This routine is to be performed three times per week, to allow the forty-eight to ninety-six hours needed for recovery and growth of the body's skeletal muscles. If you are not feeling up to working out every other day, then chances are you have become stronger and consequently are making greater inroads into your recovery ability. In such instances, extend your recovery periods between workouts to two days, working out just once every third day (e.g., Monday, Thursday, Sunday, etc.). This will give you the seventy-two hours between workouts that your advanced strength necessitates for adequate subsystem recovery and muscle-mass increases.

It is essential to work hard at these six exercises, because your results will be directly proportionate to your effort. Every repetition of every set should be raised in two seconds, held in the position of full muscular contraction for an additional two seconds, and then lowered slowly back to the starting position in four seconds. This cadence will ensure that it is the responsibility of your muscles, rather than momentum, to move the weights and will greatly enhance your results from training. When the guide number of repetitions can be reached in good form, increase the resistance by 5 percent and then try for the guide number of repetitions again.

The routine presented in this chapter, coupled with a well-balanced diet, will provide all of the muscle growth you should ever want, but it requires hard work and dedication to succeed. There is no pleasure to be found in this sort of training; the pleasures lie in the results of having trained: better strength and health. They are results that you alone have attained through the consistent application of your will and reason. You will learn of the pleasure that attends having forged your body in the fire of your will—and this is the hallmark of the true bodybuilder.

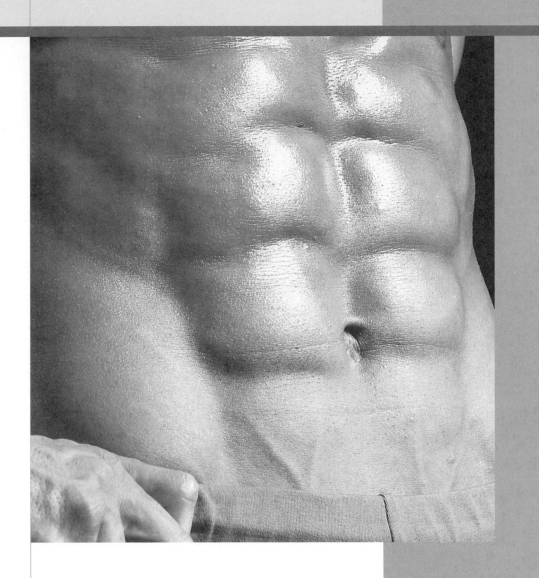

PART 3

Specialization and Refinement

9

Setting Up Your Year-Round Training Schedule

It's important to take periodic breaks from high-intensity training throughout the year in order to fully recharge your muscles and your motivation. During these off periods you may wish to expand your life experience with activities such as music or martial arts.

Now that you've adopted solid fundamentals for your training routine and been introduced to several varieties of techniques, we can look toward the high-intensity training that will produce the most significant results. First, though, to make sure you have the level of dedication required to attain your goals, we must address one of the biggest obstacles to proper training: boredom.

Many of us become bored with training. You're no doubt familiar with the feeling: you know that you should train, and yet, just the thought of training seems to fill you with inertia. This is a normal psychological response to a redundant stimulus.

We all know that from boredom does not proceed motivation, and without motivation you cannot train in a high-intensity fashion. If you cannot train in a high-intensity fashion, you will never progress toward your goals of muscular growth and bodily perfection. So, how does one stave off the eventuality of lethargy in one's training career?

PREVENTING BOREDOM AND GAINING MULTIPLE BENEFITS

The answer is subtle, though dramatic in its impact: simply alter your routine from month to month. Nothing major is required, just marginal variations on the same high-intensity theme. How does one perform these subtle variations? The answer to that query is through monthly specialization. Since boredom and overtraining march in lockstep, we prevent one by preventing the other—while at the same time stimulating almost unbelievable growth in select bodyparts every month.

The key to year-round training and, more important, year-round results is specialization. Select one bodypart to be specialized on per month, making sure to include all bodyparts throughout any twelve-month period. Keep your sets for the targeted bodypart to a maximum of five in order to maintain an adequate degree of intensity for growth inducement. Any more sets than this will require you to reduce your intensity levels in order to complete them—a step in the wrong direction if your objective is a muscular mass increase. Also, perform only one set, maximum, for the remainder of your bodyparts. This will instill a degree of intensity sufficient to induce overall growth of the body's muscular systems, will be sufficiently brief to prevent overtraining, and will be sufficiently diverse to prevent you from falling into the doldrums of boredom.

1. Never work out more than three times per week; often, working out twice in a week will produce better results.

2. Train your whole body in each session.

3. Never perform more than twelve sets in any given workout. Intermediates should perform only ten total sets in any given workout.

4. When specializing, beginners should perform only five sets for the bodypart being specialized on, with each set being a legitimate "all-out" effort. Intermediates should reduce their sets for the targeted muscle group to a maximum of three.

5. Work the specialized bodypart first in the routine, when your energy level is highest, and then train your other bodyparts in descending order—from the largest to the smallest.

6. Perform negatives on your last workout of the week (i.e., on Friday's workout).

7. Take one full week off from weight training every ten weeks.

8. When not specializing, use the basic routine described in this chapter for impressive, balanced muscular growth.

9. When specializing, select a different bodypart every month. This imparts balanced development and prevents overtraining of a muscle group.

Sample Year-Round Workout Schedule

January: General workout (total body)

February: Deltoid specialization

March: Leg specialization—quadriceps, hamstrings, calves; in mid-March take one week off from weight training and engage in only mild exercise, such as aerobics

April: Arm specialization

May: Back specialization, inclusive of trapezius

June: Chest specialization; take the first week of June off from weight training and engage in only mild exercise, such as swimming, biking, and running

July: General workout (total body)

August: Deltoid specialization; during the third week of August abstain from all forms of weight training and perform only aerobic activities

September: Leg specialization

October: Arm specialization

November: Back specialization; take the first week of November off from weight training and perform whatever form of aerobic exercise you prefer

December: Chest specialization

This schedule should serve you as a guide in setting up your own training blueprint for the coming year. It is important to take one full week off after every ten weeks of high-intensity training. This will help to keep both your enthusiasm and energy reserves primed to a high degree, thus defeating the demons of boredom and overtraining that always rear their objective-defeating heads around the ten-week mark.

Once a week, perform all of your exercises in a negative-only fashion. Negatives as a method for doing chin-ups were cited in Chapter 8. Negatives require you to perform exercises with 40 percent more weight than you normally would use and have your training partner (or partners, depending upon your strength level and the amount of weight you will be using) lift the weight to the top while you concentrate on lowering it, taking at least eight seconds to lower the resistance back to the starting position. Continue lowering the resistance until you can no longer control the descent of the weight, as when it now descends in two seconds as opposed to the initial eight.

Also keep in mind that during your "week off" you should be performing some form of aerobic activity in order to burn calories and prevent the expansion of your body's fat cells. Any activity you choose should be of very low intensity and somewhat enjoyable, such as jogging, distance walking, badminton, swimming, dance, martial arts, or bicycling. Because of the lower intensity of these activities, you will not make major inroads into your body's recuperative subsystems, thereby leaving them ample time to build up in anticipation of the following week's assaults, and the activities will burn up calories that would otherwise be stored as adipose. The formula might appear as follows: ten weeks of all-out training with emphasis on a particular bodypart to build size, and one week of endurance or aerobic training to "rip up."

If you couple this program with a balanced, calorie-reduced diet, you will look and feel better than you ever have before. When you think about it, that is why we started bodybuilding, isn't it? And now, let's get started with month one.

THE GENERAL (BASELINE) ROUTINE: OVERVIEW

We can deduce from the foregoing information that our ideal baseline routine should be intense (and, ipso facto, brief) enough to stimulate muscular growth and infrequent enough to allow for growth to take place once it has been stimulated. Ergo, the three-day-per-week system of training. What follows, then, is a whole-body, year-round routine. In the coming months, we will get into specialization on various bodyparts, should you feel so inclined, that will produce stunning gains in muscular body weight.

If you crave variety in order to keep motivated, or if certain bodyparts begin to lag, you can rely on the following chapters for advice on how to overcome these obstacles to continuous muscular progress.

Repetition Revelation

Until the mid-1980s nobody knew with any degree of certainty how many repetitions an individual should perform in a given exercise to facilitate maximum growth of specific muscle groups. "Do five repetitions for bulk" was a common statement, although

an invalid one, as we shall see; or "You've got to do twenty repetitions in the squat to make any gains from the movement whatsoever." These statements and thousands like them have been shown to be absurd in light of a major physiological discovery revealed in 1986 by Arthur Jones, of Nautilus Sports/Medical Industries.

Use of the then supremely sophisticated Nautilus medical machines (later used as the template for the MedX line of rehabilitation equipment) revealed that, in terms of repetitions, what works for one individual may not necessarily work for another. Not only does each individual have specific repetition requirements, but each of the individual's muscle groups might as well. For instance, one individual may need to perform only five repetitions in the squat to thoroughly stimulate the leg muscles into maximum growth, whereas five repetitions for another individual may do nothing in the way of stimulating growth because the repetitions were inadequate for making any meaningful inroad into the muscular reserves.

The "ideal" inroad for maximum growth stimulation was determined by these same machines to be 20 percent for all human beings. However, the number of repetitions required to induce this level of inroad into the muscular reserves will vary from person to person depending on the person's neuromuscular efficiency—the number of muscle fibers that can be recruited by the brain during a single skeletal-muscle contraction. Some people will be able to hit the 20 percent mark with a low number of repetitions; these people will have a high neuromuscular efficiency. Others will not be able to make a 20 percent inroad with anything less than perhaps fifteen to twenty repetitions; they will have a low level of neuromuscular efficiency.

Therefore, it is obvious that no one can tell you, as an individual, how many repetitions you should be doing to stimulate maximum growth. People can tell you, as I have, what the ideal percentage of inroad is, but short of determining through individual analysis what your individual specific repetitions (I.S.R.) range per muscle group is, they can tell you no more. That leads to the question of how to determine what one's "ideal repetition range" per muscle group is. Fortunately, you don't have to sell your house in order to afford a series of MedX or Nautilus medical machines to obtain the answer to your muscular queries. The solution lies in the method born of the technology and not in the technology itself.

How to Calculate Your Individual Specific Repetitions (I.S.R.)

The following four-step procedure can help you arrive at the ideal repetition range for each muscle group.

1. Determine what your maximum poundage is for a single exercise in good form, and then, after a brief rest of perhaps five minutes, perform as many repetitions as possible in good form with 80 percent of that one-rep-max weight. For example, if your one-rep max on the bench press is 200 pounds, 80 percent is 160.

2. Multiply the number of repetitions you perform by .15, and round off the result to the nearest whole number. So, if you get six reps, it's $6 \times .15 = 0.9$, or 1.

3. Add the number you have just calculated to the number of repetitions that you were able to perform. In this case, $1 + 6 = 7$ repetitions. That number becomes the high end of the rep range—that is, the number of reps for which you should shoot before increasing your resistance by 5 percent.

4. Subtract that same number, 1, from the number of repetitions you were able to perform—that is, $6 - 1 = 5$. That's now the low end of your rep range for this particular muscle group—that is, the minimum, or starting, number of repetitions for which you should shoot to stimulate a 20 percent inroad into your muscular reserves.

By this simple procedure, you can now determine the ideal repetition range for each particular muscle group to be trained (e.g., chest: five to seven repetitions). Repeat this method for all remaining muscle groups to determine their "ideal" repetition range, and then apply the resulting information to the following routine for maximum results.

1. **Barbell squats:**
2 sets of I.S.R.

2. **Lat pull-downs:**
2 sets of I.S.R.

3. **Dumbbell bench presses:**
2 sets of I.S.R.

4. **Shoulder presses:**
2 sets of I.S.R.

5. **Standing barbell curls:**
2 sets of I.S.R.

6. **Parallel bar dips:**
2 sets of I.S.R.

The Routine Explained

Warm up: Do one to five minutes of deep knee bends, stretching, mild exercise, or stationary bike—the purpose of which is to reduce viscosity to the joints, the knee in particular, so that there is no resulting trauma to the joints when you commence with the routine.

1. **Barbell squats:** Stand erect with a barbell across your shoulders and take a deep breath. With full lungs, bend your knees and lower your body until you are in a full squat position; you should be slightly below a ninety-degree angle to your shins. As soon as you reach the bottom position, rise immediately—but under control—while at the same time exhaling, so that you will be ready for a breath at the completion of the movement. Breathe in and go down for a

Dumbbell bench press—Finish position.

second repetition and so on until you have completed your set.

2. **Lat pull-downs:** Grab the lat pull-down bar with a palms-under grip, so your arms are fully extended above your head. Slowly contract your lats by pulling the bar down to your chest. Hold this position of full muscular contraction for a two-count before allowing the weight to return in four seconds back to the starting position.

3. **Dumbbell bench presses:** To perform the exercise properly, lie on a bench with two dumbbells at arm's length over your chest.

Slowly lower the dumbbells to your upper chest. Once the dumbbells have touched your chest, slowly press them back up to the top position, and repeat the procedure for the required number of repetitions. Put the weights down, rest briefly, and then perform your next exercise.

4. **Shoulder presses:** This exercise can be performed with a barbell, dumbbells, or with a machine. In order to perform this exercise properly, you should clean (remember our definitions section in the Chapter 1) the barbell to your upper chest, or to the front of your shoulders. Then, slowly press the weight upward until your arms are fully extended over your head. Slowly lower the resistance back down to your shoulders (the starting position), and repeat the procedure for the required number of repetitions. Rest briefly, and then move on to your next exercise.

5. **Standing barbell curls:** Stand erect with a shoulder-width grip on the barbell and your palms facing front. Your arms should be fully extended so that the barbell is directly in front of your thighs. Slowly curl the barbell up to shoulder height, solely using the muscles of the upper arm by bending the elbows. From this fully contracted position, slowly lower the resistance back to the fully extended (or starting) position. Repeat for the required number of repetitions, and then rest briefly before performing your next exercise. Remember to let *only* the upper arms do the work during this movement.

Shoulder press—Finish position.

6. **Parallel bar dips:** Stand between two parallel bars. Place your hands on the bars and slowly press yourself upward with your arms locked out. Now slowly lower yourself by bending your arms until you are as low as you can descend. Repeat for your I.S.R.

What is important about this routine is not so much the exercises themselves but how the exercises are performed. As for how each exercise is executed, simply follow the explanations provided throughout the book. Always attempt to add another repetition to your first set until you have reached the upper guide number within

Parallel bar dip—Start position.

Parallel bar dip—Finish position.

your repetition framework. It is not a lot of work, but the object is not to see how much exercise your body can stand; that would be endurance training and not strength training. The goal is to see how little exercise is required to stimulate maximum muscle growth.

Perform all of your exercises slowly. As I have instructed throughout this book, lift the weight in two seconds and lower it in four. Hold the fully contracted position for a two-count before you begin to lower the weight. Also make sure that your form is immaculate—exaggeratedly so, in fact. This will place more tension on the muscles and thereby raise the intensity of the exercise, which is a step in the right direction.

This high-intensity routine should be performed in less than forty-five minutes. Every time you are able to reach the upper guide number of repetitions in good form, increase the weight by 5 percent and aim for that guide number of repetitions once again.

TIME IS ON YOUR SIDE

That, in its brevity, is the routine. It is brief, but it is so of necessity. You do not need more exercise than this to stimulate maximum gains in muscular mass. If you are drastically underweight, this routine coupled with a high-calorie diet should put on up to twenty pounds in one month. If you are an intermediate, you can expect to increase your muscular bodyweight by a minimum of eight pounds. Remember that the closer you are to a "normal" weight for your height, the slower the acquisition of muscular body weight will be.

If you have been following the routines in this book on a monthly progression from the first chapter, or if you've decided to jump into the program here and were previously using a different training system, I advise taking a solid week off from training in order to recover. Then resume this program three times per week and expect to gain muscular mass at a rate so unprecedented that you may be floored.

In time, when you have effectively doubled your strength on this program, only two weekly workouts will be required, and later, only one weekly workout. The reason is that your ability to generate intensity will become so great that you will require those additional days off to merely recover, and then more time still in order to grow. (Remember the three-phase nature of the muscle-growth process.) This isn't the exclusive domain of the Arnold Schwarzeneggers of this world. When Arnold doubles his strength, he may well be capable of lifting a small apartment building, but that doesn't mean that until you are capable of similar feats you should continue to work out three days per week.

Strength is a purely relative attribute. Sure, Arnold could out-bench-press me any day of the week, but then power lifters such as Ed Coan or Bill Kazmier could out-bench Arnold any minute of the day. As soon as *you* have doubled *your* strength, it is time for a reduction in workout frequency.

This basic program will serve you well for the rest of your training life. It will produce significant results and will save you from wasting considerable time as well. I mentioned at the beginning of this book that the champions of today are champions because of heredity. If you have similar potential, this routine will realize it. If you do not, no routine will make you a champion, but the goal to realize your fullest potential remains the same. In any event, potential being the expression of possibility, you will never know if you are capable of developing a physique of Mr. Olympia proportions unless you make the attempt.

10

Specialization: Shoulders

This is the month in which we begin our specialization process, starting with the deltoids, or shoulder muscles. The shoulders, when well developed, are among the most impressive of the body's muscles.

The deltoids are composed of three heads that, collectively, resemble an inverted triangle. (The name derives from *delta*, the fourth letter of the Greek alphabet, and means "triangle-shaped.") Each of the three heads has a distinct function: the lateral head, the most impressive in terms of shoulder width, is responsible for abduction, or moving the arm away from the body in a lateral arc; the anterior head raises the arm forward and upward; and the posterior head is engaged whenever you draw your elbows backward behind your shoulders.

WHY SPECIALIZE?

In addition to dissipating the monotony that inevitably follows whenever you lock yourself into any activity for a prolonged period, specialization allows you to really blast a stubborn bodypart into renewed growth without overtraining. No more than a total of twelve sets will be performed for the whole body in any workout—inclusive of three to five sets maximum for the bodypart that is targeted for specialization that month.

Beyond the motivation factor discussed in Chapter 9, the body quickly becomes used to a repeated stressor and begins to adapt to it, so that in time, the physiological response to the routine becomes virtually nonexistent. In the vernacular, this is known as becoming "stale" from a routine. Specialization, properly done, will rid you almost indefinitely of the scourge of becoming stale. In the previous chapter I outlined how to set up various specialization routines on a month-to-month basis, as well as when to return to the basic routine, how many sets and reps to perform, and, equally important, when to schedule extracurricular activities and layoffs.

Now that we understand the need for specialization or variety in training, let us select the best exercises for overdeveloping the shoulders, the target of our first month of specialization. Because function dictates selection, we will be examining only exercises that stress the deltoids individual function. The exercises that do the best job of stressing any particular muscle group are the ones that are best able to isolate the muscle in question.

Our routine, then, will comprise isolation exercises for the targeted bodypart and, for variety, training the remaining bodyparts with a mixture of isolation and compound exercises. There will not be more than five total sets performed for your shoulders. As stated previously, performing any more than the listed number of sets will mean that you are working beneath your capabilities. Remember, making your workouts easier (i.e., longer) will result in reduced progress. Having performed your three to five all-out sets for your shoulders, you then perform seven to nine additional sets to exercise the rest of your body. Again, do not add more sets to those listed. The program as given *will produce results*, whereas adding sets or exercises will only work against your overall goals.

I can now hear you protesting, "But my arms [or legs] need more than one crummy set to stimulate growth in them!" They really do not—*if* you work like hell during that one set, utilizing proper form on all exercises and taking each set to at least a point of positive muscular failure, and then, once a week, perform a negative-only workout for your body, including the specialization exercises. Besides, when the month for arm or leg specialization arrives, you will have the opportunity to indulge in those bodyparts. (And what routines they are!)

EXERCISE PERFORMANCE IS THE KEY

This routine, like the baseline routine itemized in Chapter 9, is to be performed three times per week—Monday, Wednesday, and Friday—with a minimum of forty-eight hours elapsing between these workouts. Your performance of the exercises is the key to unlocking the door to the results you seek. If your form is sloppy and you use a lot of momentum to lift the weight, instead of muscular contraction, you can expect little in the way of results. You must become a purist for perfect exercise performance. All in all, one properly performed repetition should take you seven to eight seconds to complete. This may require a considerable drop in the poundage that you are currently using—but so what? If your muscles cannot lift the weight—as opposed to throwing it—then you're not fooling anyone by continuing to pretend that your muscles are stronger than they really are.

The first step toward becoming stronger is admitting your weakness. Once you have done that, all that remains is to overcome it. And if deltoids are your weakness, you will now have the wherewithal to overcome this malady.

THE ROUTINE

Calculating your own I.S.R. was fully explained in Chapter 9. A *breakdown* set is when you perform an exercise to the point of muscular failure, whereupon you reduce the amount of weight by 10–20 percent and immediately perform a second set.

1. Bent-over laterals:
1 breakdown set of I.S.R.

2. Side lateral raises:
1 breakdown set of I.S.R.

3. Forward raises:
1 set of 1.S.R.

4. Barbell squats:
1 set of I.S.R.

5. Calf raises:
1 set of I.S.R.

6. Palms-up chin-ups:
1 set of I.S.R.

7. Dumbbell flyes:
1 set of I.S.R.

8. Upright rows:
1 set of I.S.R.

9. Seated French presses:
1 set of I.S.R.

10. Standing barbell curls:
1 set of I.S.R.

The shoulders are worked first, while you have the most energy available to apply to them. Normally, of course, you would work the larger muscle groups, such as the legs or back, first in the routine for this same reason, but this is specialization month for shoulders, so they get priority-one treatment. The remaining seven sets for your other bodyparts will also be growth inducing if you give them (as you should) your absolute all every time.

The Routine Explained

1. Bent-over laterals: See Chapter 7 for a full description of this exercise. Repeat for your individual specific number of repetitions. When you can no longer complete a full repetition in perfect form, put down the dumbbells and immediately pick up a lighter pair, with no rest in between. Repeat the exercise with the lighter dumbbells for your I.S.R. Rest just long enough to catch your breath, and then move on to the next exercise.

Side lateral raise—Finish position.

2. Side lateral raises: This exercise effectively isolates and stimulates the lateral head of the deltoid to impart that highly sought-after appearance of width. Hold the dumbbells at your thighs, with your body perfectly erect and your back straight. Smoothly, with lateral head output only and with your elbows locked, begin to raise the dumbbells to a height just above shoulder level. Hold the resistance there for a distinct pause, and then lower the dumbbells slowly back to the starting position. Repeat for your I.S.R., and then put the dumbbells down and immediately pick up a lighter pair and, without resting, perform a second set. Again, rest just long enough to catch your breath, and then pick up yet another set of dumbbells to perform the following exercise.

3. Forward raises: Ideally, you should perform this exercise with your shoulders against a wall or a post and never allow them to leave this surface until your set is terminated. Once you have positioned yourself, grasp the dumbbells and hold them just in front of your thighs, with your arms perfectly straight. Slowly begin to raise the resistance, making sure that the anterior deltoid is the prime mover. Raise the weight in two seconds, hold the contracted position for two more seconds, and then lower the dumbbells in unison, slowly, to a count of four seconds. Repeat for your I.S.R. until you can no longer perform a full movement.

4. Barbell squats: Doing squats after having just completed your shoulder work

Forward raise—Finish position.

is mighty hard to psyche up for—but do it anyway. Squats are a particularly productive exercise for a considerable number of muscle groups. The reason we all (with the possible exceptions of Tom Platz and Paul Anderson—two athletes with exceptional thigh mass and strength who loved to squat heavy during their competitive careers) hate to do them is the very reason they are so productive: they are, to understate things, a little on the difficult side. Nevertheless, the harder you push yourself on this exercise, the greater will be your bodybuilding progress. Besides, it's only for one set—one brutal set, but still only one set just the same. So, suck it up and give it your absolute all for one perfect set of your I.S.R. The same repetition protocol followed for your shoulders, and for all bodyparts, should be followed for squats: two seconds up and four seconds down.

5. **Calf raises:** A calf raise machine is a big help for this exercise but is not essential. If you do not have access to a standing calf raise machine, grab a dumbbell and walk to the nearest steps. Stand on the step so that your heels are hanging down over the edge. Take the dumbbell in your left hand and lift your right foot off of the step, thereby transferring all of your body's weight onto your left foot. Slowly, from this fully stretched position, press the ball of your foot into the edge of the step so that your left heel begins to rise. (You should be on the very tip of your toes on that foot when in the fully contracted position.) When you reach the apex of your heel's ascent, hold the fully contracted position for a two-count before lowering the resistance slowly to the count of four. Repeat for your I.S.R., and then transfer the dumbbell to your other hand and transfer your weight to your other foot, and repeat the exercise for your I.S.R.

6. **Palms-up chin-ups:** Grasp the chin-up bar with a palms-up grip. Slowly begin to contract the muscles in your arms and try to touch the bar to your chest when you have reached the top of your ascent. Hold this contracted position for a two-count and then lower yourself slowly (in four seconds) back down to a fully stretched position. Repeat for your I.S.R.

7. Dumbbell flyes: Grab two fairly heavy dumbbells (remember that "heavy" is relative) and lie faceup on a bench. Slowly lower the dumbbells from an overhead position in an outward arc until they are a bit below chest level. Pause for one or two seconds, and then begin to slowly raise the dumbbells back to the starting overhead position in the same outward arc. (The movement should resemble your hugging a barrel.) Repeat for your I.S.R.

8. Upright barbell rows: Place your hands about six inches apart on a barbell with an overhand grip (your palms should be facing your thighs). Keeping your body straight and stationary, slowly pull the weight up to your clavicles (collar bone). Keep the barbell in close, and then slowly, in four seconds, lower it back to the starting position. See Chapter 2 for a full description and the benefits of this exercise. This exercise will also stress your depleted deltoid muscles in addition to your trapezius, teres major, infraspinatus, biceps, and forearm muscles. Hold the fully contracted position for a two-count, and then slowly lower the resistance back to the starting position to the count of four. Repeat for your I.S.R.

9. Seated French press: Discussed in Chapter 8 with an E-Z bar, this exercise can also be done with a dumbbell. To do so, take hold of the dumbbell with both hands and sit on a bench. Now hoist the dumbbell overhead, and position both of your hands beneath the uppermost plate. With your elbows stationary, slowly lower the dumbbell behind your head until your triceps are completely stretched. Pause, and then begin to press the weight back up to the starting position while keeping your elbows motionless and next to your ears. Repeat for your I.S.R. until momentary muscular failure.

10. Standing barbell curls: Nearly every bodybuilder has performed this exercise at one time or another, despite its limitations. The basic movements should be common knowledge and were described in the first chapter. Keep in mind that the curl itself should take approximately two seconds to perform. Hold the contraction for two seconds, and then lower the resistance in four seconds back down to the starting position. Repeat for your I.S.R.

The routine should be completed in less than one hour. Science has shown that brief, highly intensified workouts are the basis to realizing your muscular potential. This routine is both. As a result, it's physiologically guaranteed to stimulate maximum increases in both size and strength, which will vary according to each person's genetic potential.

11

Specialization: Legs

When I was much younger, my father told me, "Legs are the athlete's second heart." I had no idea what the hell he was talking about and just nodded my head in apparent agreement because, well, he was my dad; he was older and, so it stood to reason, much wiser than I on such matters (although this very point would be the subject of a good many debates between the two of us!).

Afterward, I dismissed this profound declaration as the ramblings of a running fanatic, which my father was, having "almost" made the Canadian Olympic team back in 3 B.C. or some such archaic date. It has only been since I began to study the disciplines of physiology and kinesiology a little more seriously that I have been able to decipher the considerable wisdom contained within my late father's maxim. You likely will never see a champion athlete in any sport with weak legs. Boxers are said to be "past their prime" when their legs weaken or become "rubbery." The same is true in baseball, soccer, football, hockey, and skiing. Bodybuilding is no different. In fact, unlike with the other sports, weak legs are immediately noticeable in bodybuilding and can destroy the symmetry that is the hard-fought hallmark of the competitive bodybuilder.

What awaits you in this chapter is a particularly effective leg-training routine. If you aren't afraid to really pile on the weight or to push yourself (after all, you have to endure it for only one month), you will reap some quick and impressive results. Your legs truly are your "second heart," and if you train them hard, your longevity in the sport of bodybuilding will be underpinned.

BUT FIRST, A LITTLE ANATOMY AND KINESIOLOGY

Excluding the calves, there are twelve muscles that make up the leg and that should be trained if complete leg development is your goal. On the frontal thigh reside a group of four muscles known as the quadriceps. The quadriceps comprises the vastus lateralis, vastus intermedius, vastus medialis, and rectus femoris. The vastus lateralis is located on the outer side of the thigh, while the vastus medialis is on the inner, or medial, side. Just above the

kneecap and between both of these muscles is the vastus intermedius, and above that is the rectus femoris, which fans out from the middle of the thigh and gets wider near its origin at the hip. All of the tendons attached to the quadriceps cross the knee joint. When they're completely contracted, the shin extends and the leg straightens. Therefore, a leg extension exercise is best for training these muscles and is included in this specialization routine.

Five separate muscles compose the inner thigh area. The largest of these is the adductor magnus, which originates on the pubis bone and inserts along the entire length of the femur, or thigh bone. When the adductor magnus is contracted, it, along with the other four medial thigh muscles, will draw the legs from a spread-out position to a position in which they are crossed. Such a movement from an open position to a closed position is called adduction.

To my recollection, Nautilus was the first machine company to provide effective resistance for these five muscle groups with its hip adduction machine, which was introduced to the general public in January 1980. By now, many other companies have similarly designed machines of varying levels of quality that will train this muscle group, and you will need to use one, as barbells and leg extension machines don't provide effective resistance to these muscles.

Finally, we come to the hamstring muscles, which compose the back of the thigh. This is the area that is probably the most underdeveloped on all bodybuilders, including those in the professional ranks.

The hamstrings comprise three separate muscles: the semitendinosus, the semimembranosus, and the biceps femoris. The tendons of the hamstrings cross over the back of the knee capsule and cause the knee to bend when contracted. Only one exercise will effectively stimulate this extremely important muscle group—the leg curl.

THE ROUTINE

1. Leg extensions:
   2 × I.S.R.

2. Adductions:
   2 × I.S.R.

3. Leg curls:
   2 × I.S.R.

4. Standing calf raises:
   2 × I.S.R.

5. Machine pull-overs:
   1 × I.S.R.

6. Dumbbell shrugs:
   1 × I.S.R.

7. Side lateral raises:
   1 × I.S.R.

8. Pec decks:
   1 × I.S.R.

9. Dumbbell kickbacks:
   1 × I.S.R.

10. Sustained (Max Contraction) chin-ups:
   1 × I.S.R.

11. Crunches:
   1 × I.S.R.

The Routine Explained

1. Leg extensions: Sit at a leg extension machine and place your feet behind the roller pads so that your knees are snug against the seat. Keeping your head and shoulders straight, slowly straighten both legs until you reach the fully contracted position. Pause briefly, and then lower under control. Repeat for your I.S.R. Immediately reduce resistance

Leg extension—Start position.

Leg extension—Finish position.

Leg curl—Start position.

Leg curl—Finish position.

by 20 percent and perform another I.S.R. set before moving on to your next exercise.

2. Adductions: Sit at the adduction machine (Nautilus or other) and place your knees and ankles on the movement arms in a spread-legged position. Make sure that your inner thighs and knees are firmly against the resistance pads, and keep your head and shoulders against the back of the seat. Slowly pull your knees toward each other, pulling with the thighs and not the lower legs, until your knees are as close together as possible. Once you've touched your legs together, hold this fully contracted position briefly, and then lower the resistance slowly back to the starting position. Repeat for your I.S.R. Immediately reduce the resistance by 20 percent and repeat for another I.S.R. set before moving on to your final leg exercise.

3. Leg curls: Lie facedown on the leg curl machine and place your feet under the roller pads, with your knees just over the edge of the bench. Slowly curl your lower legs up until they're almost touching your buttocks. Once in this fully contracted position, hold the contraction for a two-count, and then lower the resistance slowly back to the starting position. Repeat for your I.S.R., and then reduce the weight by 20 percent and perform a second I.S.R. set.

At this point in the routine, your legs are bound to feel rather wobbly—and with good reason! Nevertheless, you still have the rest of your physique to deal with, and we'll train it with only one I.S.R. set per bodypart with the following exercises:

4. **Calves: Standing calf raises.** Step underneath the shoulder pads of a standing calf raise machine so that your heels are on the required block and almost touching the ground. From this position of full stretch, slowly contract your calves until you are completely up on your toes. Hold this position for a two-count before lowering yourself in four seconds back to the starting position.

5. **Lats: Machine pull-overs.** Adjust the height of the machine so that the shoulder joint is in line with the raised portion of the plastic in front of the cam. Assume an upright position and fasten the seat belt tightly. Press the foot pedal until your elbows are resting on the pads at about chin level. Your hands should be open (on some machines you will be required to grip handles—don't grip them too tightly as a tight grip can cause your blood pressure to increase unnecessarily). Remove your legs from the foot pedal and take four seconds to slowly rotate your upper arms down and as far back as possible. Pause for two seconds in this fully contracted position and then in four seconds return your arms to the stretched position. Repeat for the required number of repetitions.

6. **Traps: Dumbbell shrugs.** Grab two heavy dumbbells and straighten your back so that the weights are in front of your thighs. Slowly contract your traps so that your shoulders begin to ascend toward your ears. When the weights have been raised as high as they can go, hold the contraction for a two-count, and then lower the weights slowly, in four seconds, back to the starting position.

7. **Delts: Side lateral raises (dumbbells).** With your body held erect, grasp two dumbbells at your thighs. Smoothly, with lateral head output and your elbows locked, raise the dumbbells to a height just above shoulder level. Hold the resistance for a distinct pause, and then lower the dumbbells slowly back to the starting position. Repeat for your I.S.R., and then put the dumbbells down and immediately pick up a lighter pair. Without resting, perform a second set with the lighter pair of dumbbells. When completed, rest just long enough to catch your breath. Pick up yet another set of dumbbells to perform the following exercise.

8. **Pecs: Pec decks.** Adjust the seat until the shoulders (when elbows are together) are directly under the axis of the overhead cams. Fasten the seatbelt (if your machine has one) and place your forearms behind and firmly against the arm pads. Some machines have handles instead of arm pads, in which case simply reach out and take hold of the handles. Slowly, in four seconds, push with your forearms and try to touch your elbows (or the handles) together in front of your chest. Pause for two seconds in this position and then slowly, in four seconds, return the handles to the starting position. Repeat for the required number of repetitions.

Pec deck—Start position.

Pec deck—Finish position.

9. Triceps: Dumbbell kickbacks. Grab hold of a light dumbbell with your right hand and bend forward from the waist, supporting yourself with your free hand. Slowly contract the triceps muscle in your right arm, which will result in the forearm extending beyond the midline of your body. Hold this fully contracted position for a two-count, and then lower the dumbbell slowly back to the starting position just in front of your hip. Repeat for your I.S.R.; then immediately reduce the resistance by 10 percent and perform a second set for the same arm. On completion, repeat this two-phase process with your left arm.

10. Biceps: Sustained (Max Contraction) chin-ups. Grasp the chin-up bar with a palms-up grip. Slowly begin to contract the muscles in your arms, and try to touch the bar to your lower chest when you have reached the apex of your ascent. Hold this contracted position for a two-count, and then lower yourself slowly (four seconds) back to the starting position. Repeat this procedure until at least eight repetitions have been completed. Rest for perhaps one to two minutes, and then repeat for another eight-to-twelve repetitions.

11. Abdominals: Crunches. Lie faceup on the floor with your hands behind your head. Keep your chin on your chest throughout the movement. Lift your feet up on top of a bench, with your feet together and your knees facing left and right. From this starting position, slowly curl your trunk upward toward a sitting position. Once you have ascended to a fully contracted position, hold the position for a two-count, and then lower yourself slowly back to the starting position. Repeat for your I.S.R.

All of the exercises listed place a constant stress, or tension, on the target muscle groups from beginning to end of each individual set. They are the most productive exercises possible for these muscle groups, owing to their extremely high intensity threshold.

Your workouts should be structured so as to allow for adequate recovery to take place in between workouts. As you develop, you'll find that the forty-eight hours we discussed earlier won't be sufficient recovery. Particularly with leg training, you might require anywhere from four days to two weeks. Unfortunately, there is no standard prescription for rest. The time needed varies from person to person and depends upon the amount of energy output and recovery ability.

If you follow this routine exactly as described, you will be amazed at how quickly your legs will grow bigger and stronger. Train hard, get adequate rest, eat a well-balanced diet, and get ready to grow!

Specialization: Arms

It's not surprising that bulging biceps and massive triceps, replete with clearly delineated veins of garden hose dimensions, are coveted by both the aspiring and competitive bodybuilder. The arms also are without question the most enjoyable bodypart to train because they have a high pain threshold and are easy to pump up to fantastic proportions, an important psychological spur in training.

As fun as the arms are to train, the old bromide about "too much of a good thing" is particularly apt when one is caught up in the seemingly omnipresent "pump-a-mania" mentality that most gym owners—and not a few bodybuilding magazines—tend to promote. It is easy to overtrain your arms— or any other bodypart—and cause them to actually regress in size and strength.

HOW OFTEN SHOULD THE ARMS BE TRAINED?

I once knew a bodybuilder in my old neighborhood who had the most amazing arms (in terms of development—they didn't do tricks or anything). The reputation of his grandiose limbs extended beyond the confines of the neighborhood to encompass the city of Toronto.

At the time, he was performing the standard bodybuilding routines of the day: training six days per week for twenty sets per bodypart, with each workout lasting on the order of one to two hours. His arms stretched the tape measure a full nineteen inches and then some, and they were the envy of all the members of his gym and of quite a few of the gentry who happened to pass him on the street as he walked to or from one of his "pump-a-mania" workouts. We all hastily concluded that the secret to developing big arms must lie in twenty-set workouts performed six days a week for one to two hours at a crack and, of course, in the steroids needed to sustain our recovery ability and muscular subsystems through those protracted periods of training. It appeared self-evident to us: this is exactly what this fellow did for his arms, and they were huge—case closed. Another victory for multiple sets.

Superficially, this is how it appeared. However, the aforementioned bodybuilder dropped out of sight for several years, only to resurface at a local Nautilus club. The rumors began anew: "He's bigger than

The arm muscles respond quickly to intense, brief, and infrequent training.

ever!"; "His arms look even more freakish than they did before!"; "He's *too* big!"; "He's training *differently*." This last statement jolted not only me but also all of the aspiring bodybuilders who used to train in his old gym. "Differently"? What did they mean by this? Was he doing even *more* sets? He was in a Nautilus gym: anything over two sets would be viewed as blasphemy! What the heck could he be doing "differently" that would account for his sudden improvement on his already supreme development?

As it turned out, he was indeed training differently. In fact, the "difference" in his training could be described as revolutionary. It was true that he was no longer training with twenty sets per bodypart and one- to two-hour workouts, but he was not heading in the direction of *more* work. Rather, he was so far down at the opposite end of the volume scale that the famed high-intensity proponent Ellington Darden would have kissed him! He was now training a mere three days per week and performing a total of six exercises per workout for only one set per exercise! But wait; it gets better!

Are you ready for this? His repetitions were only two per exercise! To top it off, each repetition lasted a mere thirty seconds, or a total of one minute per exercise—six total minutes of exercise per workout, for eighteen total minutes of training time per week. Talk about a major reevaluation regarding the requisites for building massive muscles! He had been on multiple sets and steroids, but he was now even *bigger* than he was before as a result of doing only six total minutes of exercise per training session.

While this phenomenon may seem surprising, it is no bolt from the blue to students of muscle physiology. In physiology classes students are taught that skeletal muscles hypertrophy more readily when they are taxed, or stressed, within their anaerobic pathways, which happen to fall within the fifteen- to sixty-second time frame. Any exercise that is carried on beyond sixty seconds utilizes more aerobic than anaerobic pathways. Consequently, the participant's endurance is increased to the cost of the person's size and strength.

This "either-or" example of physiological bifurcation is known in physiology circles as the "law of specificity." Retrospectively, we can see that the training program of the Canadian Colossus had each set terminate at the sixty-second mark: two concentric and two eccentric contractions at fifteen seconds apiece equals thirty seconds per rep, times two reps, which equals sixty seconds per set.

This total is just within the confines of the anaerobic metabolic processes.

What does all this tell us about how to train our arms for maximum muscle growth? First of all, it indicates that training more than three days per week is, at best, unnecessary. Second, it suggests that performing a high volume of exercise for any bodypart is unproductive. Such excessive exercise will make more of an inroad into your endurance reserves than into your size and strength reserves.

Should you then follow the aforementioned bodybuilder's routine of six total sets per workout with sixty seconds of continuous concentric and eccentric tension placed upon the targeted muscles? Perhaps you would be wise to do so, as it seems sound from an exercise science perspective—and it certainly yields impressive results. As we have seen in past chapters, the absolute maximum number of sets that one should perform for any bodypart targeted for specialization is five if you're a beginner, perhaps three or four if you're in the intermediate stage of development, and two if you're an advanced trainee. These are maximum figures, remember. You may require even fewer to actualize your muscular potential, but this can be objectively determined only by gauging your own muscular progress or relative lack thereof. If you're progressing in terms of size and strength, then the sets are at the right number; if you're not, then reduce your number of sets.

You will also recall from previous chapters that the body requires a minimum of forty-eight hours of rest between workouts in order to recover and grow. The body must first recover from the exhaustive effects of the workout, and only after this has fully occurred will it concern itself with additional growth. When specializing on arms, as we will this month, our workouts must be brief, intense, and infrequent, as well as focused on our showpiece muscle, the arms.

A LITTLE MORE ANATOMY

The function of the biceps muscle is twofold. Its primary function is the supination of the wrist—turning the hand until it's in a palms-up position; its secondary function is to lift the forearm to the clavicle. The biceps, therefore, cannot be worked efficiently until both of these functions have been fulfilled. Therefore, in the interest of efficient and efficacious training, there will be no use of E-Z curl bars for working the biceps this month. E-Z curl bars serve to pronate the wrist, thereby failing to fulfill the primary function of supination and negating your chances of training that muscle efficiently or thoroughly.

The function of the triceps muscle is also twofold. Its primary function is to extend the forearm, and its secondary function is to draw the arm down and past the sides of the body. Knowing these functions, it is relatively easy to select the exercises best suited for stimulating growth in these muscles.

For the biceps, the exercises that are in greatest accord with this muscle's function are close-grip chin-ups, concentration curls, cable curls, machine curls, and steep-angle Scott, or preacher, curls. For the triceps, the best are dips with the elbows close to the body, cable push-downs, bench dips, and dumbbell kickbacks.

TRAINING PRINCIPLES TO BE UTILIZED

This month there will be only two major principles utilized: straight sets carried beyond normal muscular "failure" via the inclusion of forced and negative repetitions; and descending sets, in which as soon as muscular failure is reached, the weight is immediately reduced by approximately 10–20 percent and you resume that exercise for an additional set. These principles, properly applied, will stimulate maximum growth in the arms, whereas the remainder of your bodyparts will, as usual, receive adequate stimulation from only one set each (just remember the Canadian Colossus).

THE ROUTINE

1. **Chin-ups:**
   1 set of I.S.R. carried beyond positive failure with forced and negative reps (i.e., two to three of each upon failure of positive reps)

2. **Concentration curls:**
   1 descending set of I.S.R. per arm

3. **Steep-angle preacher curls:**
   2 straight sets of I.S.R. carried beyond

positive failure with forced and negative reps

4. Dips:
1 straight set of I.S.R. carried beyond positive failure with forced and negative reps

5. Dumbbell kickbacks:
1 descending set of I.S.R. per arm (forced reps may also be applied here at the completion of your maximum number of positive reps)

6. Cable push-downs:
2 straight sets of I.S.R. carried beyond positive failure with forced and negative reps

7. Front squats on blocks:
1 set of I.S.R.

8. Leg curls:
1 set of I.S.R.

9. Calf raises:
1 set of I.S.R.

10. Dumbbell flyes:
1 set of I.S.R.

11. Dumbbell laterals:
1 set of I.S.R.

12. Stiff-legged dead lifts:
1 set of I.S.R.

The Routine Explained

1. Chin-ups: It is advisable to get yourself a set of wrist straps for this exercise, as you will find that your forearms will get quite a workout in addition to your biceps. Grasp the chin-up bar with your hands spaced about shoulder-width apart and your palms facing up. Slowly contract your biceps until your hands touch your shoulders (or as high as you can pull up), hold this contracted position for a two-count, and then lower yourself in four seconds back to the starting position. Repeat for your individual specific repetitions. When you can no longer complete a full repetition, step onto a chair that should be placed right next to you by the chin-up bar and, while still pulling with your arms, use your legs to assist you in getting to the top of the bar. Do this for 2 more repetitions. Then, using your legs, stand on the chair until your chin is over the bar and lower yourself down using arm strength alone to the bottom fully stretched position. Repeat this "negative" rep 3 more times. When you can perform the upper number of your I.S.R., increase the resistance by attaching weight to your torso and attempt to complete the lower number of your I.S.R.

2. Concentration curls: Sit on a bench and grab hold of a moderately weighted dumbbell in your right hand. Lean forward slightly so that your right elbow is tucked into the crook of your knee. Using just the contraction of the biceps muscle (no body English or momentum), slowly curl the dumbbell upward until it reaches your anterior deltoid, or frontal shoulder muscle. Slowly, in four seconds, lower the dumbbell back to the starting position. Repeat for your I.S.R.; then reduce the weight by 10 percent and immediately perform a second set for

Concentration curl—Start position.

Concentration curl—Finish position.

your right arm. On completion, repeat the process for your left arm.

3. Steep-angle preacher curls: After a brief rest of one to two minutes, prepare yourself for the final exercise in the biceps segment of this month's workout, barbell preacher curls. The bench should be steeply angled to guarantee that resistance is supplied in the fully contracted position of the movement. From a position of full extension, slowly curl the weight up to your shoulder. Hold the contraction for a distinct pause, and then lower the resistance slowly, in four seconds, back to the starting position of full extension. Repeat for your I.S.R., and then continue beyond failure with the inclusion of two forced reps and two negative reps,

making sure to lower the resistance during your negatives to the count of six to eight seconds. Your biceps should be considerably swollen at this stage, but you still have one more set to perform of this exercise. Remember to carry every set that you do to the point where you cannot contract your biceps even one inch. This increases the severity of the exercise and, consequently, its productivity. Rest for one to two minutes, and then get ready to work your triceps.

4. Dips: Stand between a pair of parallel dipping bars—or anything resembling a pair of parallel dipping bars, such as between two chairs—with your arms shoulder-width apart and your elbows locked. Slowly lower

Dumbbell kickback—Start position.

Dumbbell kickback—Finish position.

yourself until your knuckles are touching your armpits. From this ungodly position of full stretch, or extension, push yourself slowly back up to the starting position. Repeat for your I.S.R., and then continue beyond failure with two forced reps and two negative reps.

5. **Dumbbell kickbacks:** Grab a light dumbbell with your right hand and bend forward from the waist, supporting yourself with your free hand. Slowly contract the triceps muscle in your right arm—the forearm will extend beyond the midline of your body. Hold this position for a two-count, and then lower the dumbbell slowly back to the starting position. Repeat for your I.S.R.; then immediately reduce the resistance by 10 percent and perform a second set for the same arm. On completion, repeat this two-phase process with your left arm. See Chapter 5 for a description and the benefits of this exercise.

6. **Cable push-downs:** Grasp the bar with a palms-over grip. Your elbows should be planted firmly on the sides of your rib cage. Smoothly extend your arms until your elbows are completely locked out. It is important to hold this position of full muscular contraction and to be cognizant of how it feels; this is the only point in the exercise when all three heads of the triceps are contracted fully. After holding this position for a two-count, lower the resistance slowly back to the starting position. Repeat for your I.S.R., and continue beyond positive failure with the inclusion of two forced and two negative reps. Rest for one minute, and then perform a second and final set.

7. **Front squats on blocks:** This exercise is one of the greatest frontal thigh developers of all time. It was a favorite of Mr. "Hercules" himself, Steve Reeves, and he had a pair of the greatest legs in the game.

Front squat—Start position.

Front squat—Finish position.

Front squats place the stress exclusively on the frontal thigh, or quadriceps, muscles. To begin, place each hand over the barbell and on the opposite shoulder. Now raise your elbows so that they are at eye level. (Your arms should resemble the posture of a dancer from the Ukraine.) Slide your elbows under the middle of the barbell, which should ideally be set upon some squat racks or a power rack. Keep sliding your elbows forward until the barbell is resting on your anterior, or frontal, deltoids. Now lift the barbell from the racks and step back and away from the racks. Lower yourself slowly, to the count of four, to a full squat position,

so that your rear end is almost touching your heels. Then smoothly raise yourself back to the starting position. Repeat for your I.S.R.

8. Leg curls: It is important to always work the antagonistic muscle groups when you train. Failure to do so will result in imbalanced development, which, if left unchecked, could lead to serious injury. Leg curls work the biceps femoris, iliotibial tract, and plantaris tendons and muscles of the posterior thigh. During regular squats or leg presses, the hamstrings are worked almost as thoroughly as the quadriceps. However, because front squats are being performed this month, a disproportionate amount of stress is removed from the hamstrings and transferred to the quadriceps; hence, the need for direct antagonistic muscle stimulation. Lie down on the bench of a leg curl machine so that your heels are under the roller pads and your legs are fully extended. Slowly curl your lower legs upward until they are at a ninety-degree angle to your upper thighs. Hold this fully contracted position for a two-count before lowering the resistance slowly, in four seconds, back to the starting position. Repeat for your I.S.R.

9. Calf raises: The following six muscles are involved during calf raises: peroneus longus, tibialis anterior, exterior digitorum longus, gastrocnemius, soleus, and triceps surae. Press up as high as you can on your toes and hold the contraction for a two-count before lowering your heels in four seconds back to the starting position. Repeat for your I.S.R.

10. Dumbbell flyes: The primary function of the pectoralis major being to draw, or adduct, the arm toward the midline of the body, it stands to reason that the best pectoral exercise would be the one that most closely parallels that function—which means dumbbell flyes.

Grab two fairly heavy dumbbells (remember that "heavy" is relative) and lie faceup on a bench. Slowly lower the dumbbells from an overhead position in an outward arc until they are a bit below chest level. Pause for one or two seconds, and then begin to slowly raise the dumbbells back to the starting overhead position in the same outward arc. (The movement should resemble your hugging a barrel.) Repeat for your I.S.R.

11. Dumbbell laterals: From a standing position, grab two dumbbells and hold them at your sides, with your palms facing each other. Keeping your arms straight and using only your shoulder muscles, slowly lift the weight up to, and a bit higher than, shoulder level. Hold this position of full contraction for a two-count before lowering the dumbbells slowly, in four seconds, back to the starting position. Repeat for your I.S.R.

12. Stiff-legged dead lifts: Stand erect with your feet just under the barbell. Then, by bending your knees, grasp the barbell, with your hands a little wider apart than shoulder width and your knuckles facing front. Now slowly begin to stand erect, straightening your legs as you do so. Keep lifting the resistance until you're completely erect and the bar is in front of your thighs. Now slowly lower the resistance until it is back on the floor, and repeat the movement for your I.S.R. Rest briefly, and then move on to your next exercise. See Chapters 1 and 2 for a description and benefits of this exercise.

If this routine is followed under the guidelines of the principles given, you will notice a significant increase in your arm girth. To add size, use this routine plus a well-balanced but calorie-increased diet. Should you find yourself getting weaker, or having trouble recuperating between workouts, cut your weekly workouts down to two (e.g., Monday and Thursday); this will provide you with the additional recovery time that your body in this instance will require.

13

Specialization: Back

Generally, when one thinks about the back muscles, one envisions the lats, or latissimus dorsi. These muscles are responsible for the highly prized V shape that bodybuilder Steve Reeves popularized throughout his colorful career.

You may not be aware of the existence of several other back muscles, including the trapezius, intraspinatus, rhomboideus, teres minor, teres major, and erector spinae—all of which, when fully developed, impart the aura of total development to the bodybuilder's physique. For the back to be worked adequately, all of these muscles must be stressed in some way through progressive resistance exercise. That is what this chapter's routine will accomplish. First, though, we need to be cognizant of the functions of these muscles in order to select the exercises that will best induce growth stimulation.

THE BACK: FUNCTION AND DESIGN

The back is composed of many divergent muscle groups. Some, such as the teres major and latissimus dorsi, have functions that are parallel. Therefore, the proper performance of one exercise will affect several related muscle groups and, thus, save us much training time.

The trapezius muscle arises from the base of the neck and extends outward toward the shoulder blades and down to the middle of the back. Its function is to elevate the shoulders and to abduct the arm. (By "abduct," I do not mean to imply that a theft of one's arm takes place; rather, the arm is moved out and away from the midline of the body.) It is also activated whenever you draw your head backward and to either side. The best exercise for this muscle is, without doubt, shrugs, which duplicate exactly the trapezius's major function. The rhomboids' function is to draw the scapula up and inward, and so this function too is perfectly paralleled whenever shrugs are performed.

The latissimus dorsi, the real "show-piece" muscle of the upper back, and the teres major are both activated whenever you draw your arms downward, backward, or inward. The exercises that best correspond to their function, then, are any type of rowing motion, such as Nautilus or Max machine pull-overs, Max Straps pull-downs, lat machine pull-downs, bent-over rowing, or T-bar rowing. As its name implies, it is the broadest (latissimus) muscle of the back (dorsi). It extends from the sixth thoracic vertebra downward until its lowest fibers attach to the upper edge of the ilium, or hip bone. This broad, triangular muscle has its insertion along the front of the humerus, or upper-arm bone, close to its head. Whereas the deltoid raises the arm and draws it forward, the latissimus dorsi pulls the arm downward and backward.

The infraspinatus and teres minor are both activated whenever the upper arm is abducted or rotated. Any form of wide-grip pull-down or chin-up will directly stress these two muscle groups. Although the Max Contraction torso machine is the only one to stress them directly, other exercises will stress them efficaciously, such as parallel-grip pull-downs on the lat machine or any exercise that keeps your elbows out from the midline of your body, including bent-over rows.

The erector spinae muscles are activated whenever extension of the trunk takes place, as in hyperextensions, dead lifts, good mornings, side bends, Nautilus hip and back machines, Nautilus lower-back machines, and Max Contraction machines.

So much for anatomy and physiology—and now on to the routine.

THE ROUTINE

1. Chin-ups:
   1 × I.S.R.

2. Dumbbell pull-overs:
   1 × I.S.R.
   Superset with:

3. Lat pull-downs:
  1 × I.S.R.

4. Wide- or parallel-grip pull-downs:
  1 × I.S.R.

5. Barbell shrugs:
  1 × I.S.R.
  Superset with:

6. Upright barbell rows:
  1 × I.S.R.

7. Hyperextensions:
  1 × I.S.R.

8. Hack squats:
  1 × I.S.R.

9. Leg curls:
  1 × I.S.R.

10. Seated calf raises:
  1 × I.S.R.

11. Wide-grip parallel bar dips:
  1 × I.S.R.

12. Standing French presses:
  1 × I.S.R.

While there is no direct biceps work in this month's routine, the biceps are actually worked thoroughly—and, in most cases, directly—from all of the back exercises at the beginning of the workout. This is a positive omission, for several reasons. First, there will be no motive to "hold off" from performing an all-out effort on each of the back exercises, since they will be the only stimulation your biceps will receive this month. Second, any direct exercise attempted after the all-

out sets in which the biceps are involved would constitute overtraining. Finally, physiologists have recently found that the muscles that are not worked directly can sometimes, albeit briefly, hypertrophy, due to the extra time allotted for growth and recovery.

Removing the Weak Links

You will find that whenever the larger muscle groups (such as the legs, lats, or chest) are trained with compound movements, other weaker muscles (such as the lower back, biceps, and triceps) are also involved. Consequently, the weaker muscles give out before a true state of muscular failure can be reached in the larger muscle groups. This problem can be alleviated by employing the technique of preexhaustion. It calls for the performance of an isolation exercise before performance of the compound movement (i.e., one in which more than three muscle groups are involved), moving from the isolation to the compound movement with all speed.

This month the weak link will be the smaller and, ipso facto, weaker biceps muscle of the upper arms, which will give out before pure muscular failure has occurred within the latissimus dorsi of the upper back. By performing dumbbell pull-overs first, however, we will be essentially isolating the lats and thereby saving the strength of the smaller biceps muscles for our next lat exercise, lat pull-downs. This will allow the lats to be pushed beyond a state of normal muscular failure, because in this instance, the biceps will be temporarily stronger than the prefatigued lat muscles.

Likewise with shrugs and upright rows: the biceps would again be the muscle that would otherwise give out first in the performance of upright rows. By performing the isolation movement of shrugs first in the cycle, we call upon the strength of the biceps to carry the prefatigued trapezius beyond a regular state of muscular failure with the compound exercise of upright rows immediately following the performance of shrugs. Remember to move quickly from one exercise to another in a cycle. Ideally, there should be no rest at all between exercises. Even as little as three seconds of rest will allow temporary muscle recovery to occur, and the preexhaustion principle would be negated.

The Routine Explained

1. Chin-ups: To begin this exercise, reach up to grasp a wall-mounted, ceiling-mounted, or free-standing chin-up bar. Your body should be fully extended beneath the bar. Slowly, from a position of full extension, begin to contract your lats, raising yourself until your hands touch your chest. Hold this fully contracted position for a two-count before lowering yourself slowly, in four seconds, back to the starting position. Repeat for your I.S.R., and when you hit failure in this movement, either have your partner provide enough assistance for you to complete four more reps, or give yourself forced reps by standing on a stool or chair to assist you in

Chin-up (wide-grip)—Finish position. Although a close grip is preferred for all back exercises, a wide grip can be employed from time to time for variety with no ill effect.

ascending to the fully contracted position. Rest for one minute, and then begin your next back exercise.

2. Dumbbell pull-overs: Grasp a moderately weighted dumbbell in both hands and lie back on a flat bench crosswise so that only your shoulders are touching the bench. Extend the dumbbell beyond your head so that it is almost touching the floor. From this position of full stretch, and with a slight bend in your arms, slowly, with your lats as prime mover, pull the dumbbell over your head to

Lat pull-down—Finish position.

approximately your sternum. A deliberate pause in this position should precede your lowering the dumbbell back to the starting position in four seconds. Repeat for your I.S.R., and, if possible, have your partner give you two forced reps, followed by two negative reps. Then release the dumbbell, and immediately move to your next exercise.

3. **Lat pull-downs:** Grab the lat pull-down bar with a palms-under grip, so your arms are fully extended above your head. Slowly contract your lats by pulling the bar down to your chest. Hold this position of full muscular contraction for a two-count before allowing the weight to return in four seconds back to the starting position. Repeat for your I.S.R. After a two-minute rest it will be time for our final lat exercise.

4. **Wide- or parallel-grip pull-downs:** This exercise will hit the teres minor and infraspinatus muscles of the upper back, in addition to the latissimus dorsi. If you have a choice between a bar that allows you a parallel grip and one that allows only a wide grip, choose the parallel-grip bar. A parallel grip puts your biceps in a fully supinated position, which is their strongest pulling position; therefore, the biceps are not as much of a weak link to your back training as when you use the pronated grip (which places the biceps in their weakest pulling position) that a wide grip on a regular bar requires.

As in your previous set of pull-downs, grab hold of the bar and sit down. You may need some counterresistance to be applied to your legs to anchor you when the weights

Parallel-grip pull-down—Finish position.

start getting heavy. Pull the bar down to your chest, keeping your elbows pointed out to your sides. Hold the fully contracted position for a two-count before returning the resistance to the starting position in four seconds. Repeat for your I.S.R., and have your partner force out three more reps.

5. **Barbell shrugs:** Grab a heavy barbell, and straighten your back so that the weight is in front of your thighs. Slowly contract your traps so that your shoulders begin to ascend toward your ears. When the weight has been raised as high as it can go, hold the contraction for a two-count, and then lower the weight slowly, in four seconds, back to the starting position. Repeat for your I.S.R., and then proceed immediately to the following compound movement.

6. **Upright barbell rows:** Select a moderately weighted barbell, remembering that your strength will be approximately 50 percent less than it would be if you were "fresh," and position your hands so that they are no more than six inches apart. Slowly pull the barbell up toward your chin, keeping your elbows pointed outward. Once you have reached the apex of the bar's ascent, hold the position of full muscular contraction for a definite pause, and then slowly lower the bar, under control, in four seconds back to the starting position. Repeat for your I.S R., and then have your partner help you force out two more reps. Rest for one or two minutes, and then begin your next exercise.

7. **Hyperextensions:** If you have access to a special hyperextension bench like the one in the accompanying photos, use it. Otherwise, simply lie crosswise over a bench so that your torso is over the edge. Have your partner hold or sit on your legs, or in some other way place resistance on them to counterbalance the weight of your torso. In either case, place a light weight behind your neck, and bend over at the waist. Slowly raise your torso using your erector spinae muscles until you have ascended as high as possible.

Hyperextension—Start position.

Hyperextension—Finish position.

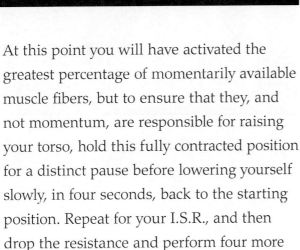

Hack squat—Start position.

Hack squat—Finish position.

At this point you will have activated the greatest percentage of momentarily available muscle fibers, but to ensure that they, and not momentum, are responsible for raising your torso, hold this fully contracted position for a distinct pause before lowering yourself slowly, in four seconds, back to the starting position. Repeat for your I.S.R., and then drop the resistance and perform four more repetitions.

8. Hack squats: This is a tremendous frontal thigh developer, and it shifts the resistance to that too often neglected area of the thigh—the vastus medialis. To begin, lean back under the shoulder pads on the hack squat machine. Now slowly push your legs until they have completely locked out. As in any locked-out position, no resistance is applied to the muscles; do not hold this position, but rather begin an immediate descent as soon as your legs have locked out. Lower yourself slowly, in four seconds,

back to the starting position. Repeat for your I.S.R., trying to maintain a constant cadence to your reps.

9. Leg curls: The action of the last exercise was entirely frontal thighs, so we shall now concentrate on working our antagonistic muscles—the biceps femoris, semitendinosus, and semimembranosus. Working these antagonistic muscle groups is important; failure to do so will eventually lead to muscle tears, pulls, and other related discomfort due to the disproportionate stress placed on the muscles. Have your partner help you in coaxing four more reps out of your hamstring muscles after you've reached your I.S.R.

10. Seated calf raises: This exercise works primarily your soleus and the outer sweep of the gastrocnemius. To begin, sit at a seated calf machine and place the resistance pads over your knees. Release the

Seated calf raise—Finish position.

Wide-grip parallel bar dip—Start position.

Wide-grip parallel bar dip—Finish position.

locking mechanism, thereby disengaging the weight, and slowly rise on the balls of your feet until your calves are in a fully contracted position. Pause in this position for a two-count, and then lower the resistance slowly, in four seconds, back down to the starting position. Make sure to really stretch your calves by trying to touch your heels to the ground whenever you lower the resistance. Repeat for your I.S.R.

11. **Wide-grip parallel bar dips:** Ideally, you should have a V-shaped dipping bar with a base of at least thirty-six inches. If you do not have access to such a bar, try to get as wide a hand spacing as possible on whatever bars or chairs you are using for your dips. Keeping your elbows pointed outward, slowly lower yourself from an arms-locked position. It should take four seconds for you to reach the bottom position, where your knuckles are as close to your armpits as you can get them (as low as you can possibly stretch). Hold this position for a brief pause, and then, with your elbows still pointed out, push yourself back up to the starting position. Repeat for your I.S.R.

12. **Standing French presses:** Grab an E-Z curl bar and press it overhead. Then, instead of lowering your elbows, keep them stationary and just lower your forearms. The bar should be lowered to a point just below the back of your neck in four seconds, and, with no momentum whatsoever, your triceps should slowly power the bar back to the arms-locked starting position. Repeat for your I.S.R., and then cheat out two more; finally, have your partner give you two negatives.

Always strive to add another repetition to your previous best attempt in this exercise. Once the guide number of repetitions has been reached (your I.S.R.), increase the resistance that you have been using by 5 percent, and aim for the lower guide number of reps again. Remember that all exercises should be performed under control by raising the resistance in two seconds, holding the contracted position for an additional two seconds, and then lowering

Standing French press—Start position.

Standing French press—Finish position.

the resistance in four seconds back to the starting position.

This workout hits every back muscle there is and has been tried and proven effective. In fact, in an experiment that I conducted in Canada some years back, one participant gained three inches on his chest-to-waist ratio. So, dig down deep, giving it all you've got, and you will be rewarded with a well-developed back.

14

Specialization: Chest

Awell-developed chest, on either sex, is arguably the most universally admired bodypart that members of our species possess. Women are concerned with ways to increase their "busts," while men are concerned with increasing their "pecs." This desire is particularly strong among teenage males. Some, in their unbridled desire to develop themselves, so overtrain their chests (among other muscles) that growth, if it comes at all, will proceed at a snail's pace. Agony and frustration then ensue, and eventually the bodybuilder gives up in despair. This needn't be the case if the correct exercises and training principles are employed by the pectorally aspiring trainee.

That brings us to two principal questions: what exercises should one choose for the purpose of developing the chest, and how does one properly perform them? This chapter's routine endeavors to answer both as well as other related questions.

THE CHEST ANATOMY AND PHYSIOLOGY

There are, in effect, three different chest muscles: the pectoralis major, pectoralis minor, and serratus anterior, or serratus magnus. Each of these must be fully stimulated as a result of your workouts if complete chest development is your goal.

The pectoralis major arises from the anterior surface of the sternal half of the clavicle, the anterior surface of the sternum, the cartilages of the true ribs, and the aponeurosis of the external oblique. By "true ribs," I refer to the anterior extremities of each of the first seven pairs of ribs that are connected with the sternum in front by means of the costal cartilages. The fibers of the pectoralis major converge and form a thick mass, which is inserted by a flat tendon into the crest of the greater tubercle of the humerus, or upper-arm bone. If the arm has been raised, the pectoralis major, acting with the latissimus dorsi and the teres major, draws the arm down to the side of the chest. Acting alone, it adducts and draws the arm across the chest, also rotating the arm inward.

The pectoralis minor is underneath and entirely covered by the pectoralis major. It arises from the upper margins and outer surfaces of the third, fourth, and fifth ribs near their cartilages and is inserted into the coracoid process of the scapula (the little bump of bone on your shoulder). The action of the pectoralis minor is to depress the point of the shoulder and to rotate the scapula downward.

The serratus anterior, or serratus magnus, arises from the outer surfaces and superior borders of the upper eight or nine ribs and from the intercostals between them. The action of the serratus is to carry the scapula forward and to raise the vertebral border of the bone, as in pushing. It also assists the trapezius in raising the acromion process and supporting weights on the shoulder, and it assists the deltoid in raising the arm.

Now, after all that, what are the best exercises for stressing the musculature of the chest? Well, given that the action of the pectoralis major is to draw the arm across the chest, the exercise that most closely parallels that function is dumbbell flyes (cable crossovers or a pec deck can also be utilized). The primary action of the pectoralis minor being to lower the upper arm down from an overhead position then pullovers and decline bench presses are the best way to activate this muscle's fibers. The serratus anterior's function is to carry the scapula forward, and consequently, it is best served by performing pull-overs. Ergo, the following three exercises will constitute the core of our chest specialization training this month:

1. Dumbbell flyes
2. Decline presses
3. Pull-overs

TRAINING PRINCIPLES

As you will recall from previous chapters, the most important factor regarding training is intensity of effort. In order to grow, you must first give your body a reason to grow. Muscle growth cannot be induced by merely repeating that which is already easy and well within your body's current capabilities. Muscle growth beyond normal levels can be induced only by maximum effort; every repetition of every set must be performed in perfect style. That is to say, every repetition must be raised in two seconds, held in the position of full muscular contraction for an additional two seconds, and then returned to the starting position in four seconds.

In all, a properly performed set of eight repetitions plus two forced reps should take a total of eighty seconds. In our specialization this month, we will once again be making use of the principle of descending sets. That is the performance of an isolation exercise first to the point of momentary contractile inability and then, after reducing the resistance by approximately 10–20 percent, immediately performing the same isolation movement again, to the point of momentary contractile inability—or to the point of positive failure, as it is referred to in the vernacular.

In addition, a negative-only set should be performed during Friday's workout (this being another Monday-Wednesday-Friday routine), in which you use approximately 40 percent more weight than you would normally be handling in your exercises. Have your training partner (or partners, depending upon your strength level) lift the weight for you while you prepare to concentrate exclusively on lowering the resistance in eight seconds. The same repetition protocol that you would use in a regular workout applies to your negative-only training—that is, as many repetitions as your I.S.R. calls for.

Monday's workout should include forced reps and negatives, but Wednesday's workout should be taken to positive failure only. As has been the rule during all types of specialization, the specialized bodypart will be addressed first in the workout with a maximum of five sets. The remainder of the bodyparts will then be covered with one set each, taken to absolute muscular failure (except for Wednesday's workout).

THE ROUTINE

1. Dumbbell flyes:
1 descending set of I.S.R.

2. Decline bench presses:
1 descending set of I.S.R.

3. Pull-overs:
2 straight sets of I.S.R.

4. Leg extensions:
1 set of I.S.R.

5. Lunges:
1 set of I.S.R.

6. Standing calf raises:
1 set of I.S.R.

7. Seated cable rowing:
1 set of I.S.R.

8. **Stiff-legged dead lifts:**

   1 set of I.S.R.

9. **Standing (supinating) dumbbell curls:**

   1 set of I.S.R.

10. **Bench dips:**

    1 set of I.S.R.

The Routine Explained

1. **Dumbbell flyes:** The semicircular motion of the arms during the performance of this exercise is said to resemble aerodynamically the motion of the wings of a bird while in flight. With the setup as detailed in Chapter 3, once the dumbbells are raised, it should take you all of four seconds to completely lower them to the sides of your chest. Hold this stretched position for a two-count before raising the dumbbells back to the starting position. Repeat for your individual specific repetitions guideline number until momentary contractile inability. Immediately reduce the weight by 20 percent, and perform a second set to positive failure.

2. **Decline bench presses:** You will need a decline bench of some sort to perform this exercise properly. Take the resistance off the uprights and hold it for a moment at arm's length. Slowly lower the resistance to your collarbone, making a conscious effort to keep your elbows wide. Pause here for a second or two, and then press the resistance back up to the starting position. Repeat for your individual specific number of repetitions and, depending on which day of the

Decline bench press—Finish position.

week your workout falls, have your partner assist by giving you two forced repetitions or two negative repetitions. Immediately reduce the resistance by 20 percent, and perform a second set of your I.S.R.

3. **Pull-overs:** Lie on a bench with a light barbell (or a centrally loaded dumbbell), held at arm's length over your chest. Maintaining the arm's-length position, slowly lower the weight until it almost touches the floor behind you. Make an effort to keep your arms locked throughout the movement, and when you inhale, attempt to draw in as much oxygen as you can while lifting the weight as high as possible. The weight is not a major factor in this exercise, whereas the degree of stretch is. After a brief respite, perform a second set of I.S.R.

4. Leg extensions: Leg extensions are unparalleled in their ability to thoroughly isolate the quadriceps muscles of the frontal thighs. Other exercises can work the quads, but none will do so as efficiently. That's because there are no "weak links" in this movement; it is powered solely by the strength of your quadriceps. As described in Chapter 5, hold the position of full contraction for a two-count before lowering the resistance in four seconds back to the starting position. Repeat for your I.S.R.

5. Lunges: Grab a moderately weighted barbell and place it across your shoulders as if you're about to squat with it. Instead of performing squats, step forward with your right leg as far as you can, until your left knee touches the ground. Pause briefly in this position before pushing with your right leg to return to your initial position. Repeat the movement right away with your left leg. Continue this movement, alternating legs, for your I.S.R. per leg. Lunges work your entire leg, but the lower you descend, the more gluteal and biceps femoris fibers are activated.

6. Standing calf raises: Step underneath the shoulder pads of a standing calf raise machine so that your heels are on the required block and almost touching the ground. From this position of full stretch, slowly contract your calves until you are completely up on your toes. Hold this position for a two-count before lowering your-

Lunge—Start position.

Lunge—Finish position.

self in four seconds back to the starting position. Repeat for your I.S.R.

7. **Seated cable rowing:** You will need a floor pulley attachment to perform this exercise properly. To begin, take hold of the handle (or handles, on some machines) and lean forward at the waist, thereby starting the movement from a position of full extension. Slowly contract your lats, thereby drawing your elbows behind your torso. When you have drawn your elbows as far

Seated cable rowing—Start position.

Seated cable rowing—Finish position.

behind you as you possibly can, hold this position of full contraction for a two-count before lowering the resistance slowly, in four seconds, back to the starting position. Repeat for your I.S.R.

8. **Stiff-legged dead lifts:** Stand erect with your feet just under the barbell. Then, by bending your knees, grasp the barbell, with your hands a little wider apart than shoulder width and your knuckles facing front. Now slowly begin to stand erect, straightening your legs as you do so. Keep lifting the resistance until you're completely erect and the bar is in front of your thighs. Again, hold the fully contracted position for a two-count before returning the weight back to the floor in four seconds. Repeat for your I.S.R.

9. **Standing (supinating) dumbbell curls:** This exercise fulfills the primary function of the biceps brachii muscle: supination. To begin, pick up two moderately weighted dumbbells and hold them at your sides. Slowly curl one of them up toward your shoulders. When you begin this exercise, your palms should be facing one another, but when the dumbbell you are curling has reached your shoulder, your palm should be facing toward your face (or at least supinated as much as possible). From this position of full contraction, slowly lower the dumbbell in four seconds, under control, back to your side. Repeat the procedure with the opposite arm. Repeat for your I.S.R.

10. Bench dips: This is actually an excellent upper-body developer, but the majority of focus is on the triceps of the upper arm. The bench you will be using should be slightly behind your back so that the secondary function of the triceps, to draw the arm down and behind the torso, is fulfilled. Place your feet on the floor in front of you, with your arms in a locked-out position on the bench behind you. From this position, slowly break the lock in your arms and lower yourself in four seconds to a position of full stretch, where your hands are almost in contact with your armpits. Just being in such close proximity to your armpits should be incentive enough to push yourself back up to the starting position, but if it's not,

Standing (supinating) dumbbell curl—Finish position.

Standing (supinating) dumbbell curl—Finish position.

Bench dip—Start position.

Bench dip—Finish position.

think of all the muscle growth you will be stimulating with each and every rep that you perform in correct style during this exercise. Repeat for your I.S.R.

That concludes this routine. Remember that the stronger you become, the greater the energy outout, and consequently, the easier it is to overtrain. That is why it may be necessary for some beginners to space their workouts out to once every three days while on this program.

If your chest development has been something less than impressive up to this point, give this month's specialization routine a try and watch your under-par pectorals become a problem of the past.

15

An Incredible Abdominal Routine

It is becoming more and more prevalent: everybody wants a "six pack" of abs. I'm not talking about just having a bodyfat level low enough to allow your abs to be visible to the undiscerning eye. No, what I'm talking about is the fixation our culture has for very well-developed abdominal muscles. The abs are, after all, skeletal muscles, and they respond to the same stimulus for development as all other skeletal muscles—high-intensity training!

In the past, many bodybuilders could get by on muscle mass alone. These days, to really look impressive, a bodybuilder must not only display good muscle mass but also be highly defined. Today's bodybuilder must combine muscular massiveness with an element of refinement, which means that every muscle group must be chiseled distinctly separate from its neighboring muscle groups, with the body's fat stores reduced to the point where the abdominal development is actually detectable. Someone whose abs are obscured by fat is not a bodybuilder but is just someone who trains with weights.

True bodybuilders look the part, which means their fat stores are at a level low enough to reveal their abdominal development—or lack thereof—at all times. This is not meant to imply that unless your abs appear to be as sharp as those of the current Mr. Olympia 365 days a year, you're deluded in considering yourself a bodybuilder. That is an unrealistic and, more important, unnatural level of muscularity that even Mr. Olympia cannot maintain for more than a couple of weeks per year.

Rather, you should always be able to see your abs—all three layers (like Steve Reeves or Bruce Lee). Then diet down even more strictly to bring out the deeper cuts when zeroing in for a contest. Allowing fat to accumulate on your body is always a negative factor. As my late friend Mike Mentzer, a former Mr. Universe winner, often pointed out: "Whenever fat is allowed to accumulate, it is going to have to be eliminated someday through undereating and overtraining—a combination that leads to the loss of muscle as well as fat."

To maintain a visible abdominal musculature, it is important to eat a well-balanced diet that contains only enough calories to maintain your existing degree of muscle mass. We are not concerned with maintaining your existing degree of bodyfat, as that is only excess baggage that will one day have to be gotten rid of.

Most of us are sporting too much adipose tissue. How, then, can we maintain our status as bodybuilders without sacrificing our hallowed muscle mass? Or, better yet, is there a way to actually increase our muscle mass while simultaneously decreasing our bodyfat stores? Well, fortunately, there is a way, owing to the fact that muscle cells and fat cells are two entirely different entities and respond to two entirely different stimuli. To increase your bodyfat stores, all you have to do is live a rather sedentary existence and eat at every opportunity. Increasing your muscle mass stores is nowhere near as easy. To stimulate your muscles to grow larger and stronger, you must first expose them to brief, high-intensity training sessions to encourage growth, and then allow them adequate time to both recover and grow from the exercise session—and then provide adequate nutrition to feed the growth-and-repair process of your body so that the growth can take place. As I said, the process is far removed from the business of gaining fat, but the rewards in health and appearance more than offset the expenditure of labor required to realize this objective.

Gaining muscle and losing fat at the same time is accomplished via brief, infrequent, high-intensity exercise that stimulates growth in the targeted muscle group (in this case our abdominals) and marrying this training regimen to a well-balanced, calorie-reduced diet.

The reduced-calorie diet (five hundred to one thousand calories below your maintenance need of calories) will cause a gradual decrease of your body's fat stores, while the high-intensity exercise stimulates a gradual increase in your muscle-mass level. The key to developing your abdominal muscles, then, is to perform low sets of high-intensity abdominal exercises and consume a low-calorie diet. I'll provide you with the ideal exercise system to develop your abdomen, but I'll leave it to you to monitor your calorie intake.

Knee-up on chin bar—Finish position.

THE ROUTINE

1. Knee-ups on chin bar:
   2 × I.S.R.

2. Crunches:
   2 × I.S.R.

3. Standing oblique crunches:
   2 × I.S.R.

The Routine Explained

1. Knee-ups on chin bar: Take hold of a chin-up bar from a dead-hang position, and slowly draw your knees up into your chest area. Try to make your knees touch your chest. Once you have reached the fully contracted position, hold this position for

a count of two, and then lower your knees slowly back to the starting position. Repeat for your I.S.R. Rest briefly, and then perform a second set of your I.S.R.

2. Crunches: You were introduced to this exercise in Chapter 1. Lie on the floor with your knees over the top of the exercise bench. With your hands clasped behind your neck, slowly draw yourself up until your shoulder blades are approximately two inches off the floor. Hold this contraction tightly for a pronounced squeeze, and then

Crunch—Finish position.

Standing oblique crunch—Start position.

Standing oblique crunch—Finish position.

lower yourself slowly back to the starting position. Repeat for your I.S.R. After a brief pause, perform a second set of your I.S.R.

3. Standing oblique crunches: Stand with your left side next to a high pulley machine. Take hold of a high pulley handle with your right hand, which should be just above your left shoulder. Keeping your right arm pinned to your torso, bend to the right using only the strength of your oblique muscles. Using a slow and controlled motion, return to the upright position, and repeat for your I.S.R. Upon completion, switch sides, taking the pulley handle in your left hand, and repeat the entire procedure for the opposite side of your torso. On completion, immediately switch sides again, and do an additional set of your I.S.R. for each side.

These exercises performed exactly as listed will set off a well-developed physique and will not—despite misinformed opinion to the contrary—thicken or expand one's waist. The breadth of your abdominal area is dictated largely by the width of your pelvic bone, which is a genetically inherited characteristic and therefore not subject to alteration.

Remember to train your abs as you would any other bodypart—with high-intensity training—and they'll respond by strengthening, improving your posture, and separating into six (the old "six pack" mentioned earlier) distinct sections. When combined with your reduced calorie intake, training will create a look that not only will turn heads on a crowded beach but also might one day provide you with that "six pack" that is so popular.

16

Dieting to Build Pure Muscle

Diet is probably the most fundamental component of the bodybuilder's makeup. The food you eat becomes the fuel that allows you to perform heavy sets of muscle-building exercise, as well as becoming the primary fuel of your nervous system and brain. All mental functions, from choosing a biceps exercise to abstract philosophical contemplation, are fueled by what you put into your mouth.

Because this aspect of bodybuilding is so fundamental, it can be broken down logically into some basic arithmetic. To start off, let's conduct an elementary caloric analysis of human tissue. It's a fact that a pound of human muscle tissue will yield about 600 calories when measured with a device known as a calorimeter, while a pound of fat will yield 3,500 calories. We will return to these numbers in a moment.

As a bodybuilder, you must strive to increase your percentage of organic muscle while simultaneously reducing your stores of bodyfat. The reward for success is a more functional and efficient (not to mention well-chiseled) physique. Unfortunately, the average bodybuilder finds it nearly impossible to gain even ten pounds of solid muscle tissue in a year's time, due largely to the person's falling prey to the hype and outright B.S. that is propagated by most bodybuilding publications and that lines the pockets of more than a few gym owners and personal trainers.

Fortunately, to reach a solution to your nutritional problems, you needn't try to sort through the dubious proclamations of the bodybuilding publishing industry (most representatives of which exist solely to sell you their products, but that's another story entirely). Instead, you need look no further than the field of nutritional science. You will quickly learn that all that is required in the course of a year to allow for ten pounds of muscle growth would be 600 (the number of calories in a pound of muscle) times 10 (the number of pounds of muscle growth stimulated in a year), or 6,000 extra calories a year over and above your present energy requirements.

EATING ITSELF ISN'T THE ANSWER

Now, just eating 6,000 extra calories above the amount you need to maintain your current body mass is no guarantee that you will grow an additional ten pounds of muscle this year. You have to train hard enough to stimulate ten pounds of growth first. Then, if the calories are present in the form of nutritious food, the growth that you have stimulated will take place.

If you take this a little further and divide the 6,000 calories a year by 365, you find that you need only 16.4 calories a day above your maintenance need of calories. For instance, let's say that you currently weigh 200 pounds and require 3,000 calories a day just to maintain that weight; that is, at 3,000 calories you don't gain or lose weight, but simply stay at 200 pounds. Then, you train with sufficient intensity to stimulate ten pounds of muscle growth, rest adequately to allow your body the time it requires to build those ten pounds of additional muscle, and consume 3,016.4 calories a day. At the end of this year you would weigh 210 pounds. Very simple.

Similar calculations can be applied to fat. Since one pound of fat contains 3,500 calories, when in the course of time you've consumed 3,500 calories over and above what you needed to maintain yourself, you'll have added a pound of fatty tissue to your body. If you require 3,000 calories a day for maintenance, but then you consume 3,500 calories a day, which is 500 more than you need, in the course of a week you would gain one pound of fat.

The same holds true for losing fat. When you burn up 3,500 calories by expending more energy than you take in as food calories, you will lose one pound of fat. This means that in order to grow muscle, you need to consume approximately one-sixth of what you would need to produce fat. If for some reason you simply wanted to become fatter, the answer is simple: eat a lot; but if you want to grow only muscle, don't eat too much above your maintenance need of calories.

If you've been stuffing your face with protein products thinking that you're forcing your muscles to use all of the "extra" protein, stop fooling yourself. The body utilizes only as much protein as it needs to maintain itself plus what little extra it might require to assist in producing the growth that you stimulated with your training efforts. Any additional protein consumed beyond this amount will be excreted at best, or stored as fat at worst. Moreover, since protein is primarily a building-and-repair nutrient, as opposed to a preferred energy source by the body, our protein requirements do not tend to increase when we perform physical activity. Instead, engaging in vigorous activity increases the need for carbohydrates, because it is the nutrient most easily converted to glucose, which, when converted to the polymer of glycogen, is the primary energy source of human muscle tissue.

Protein requirements, on the other hand, depend solely on individual body weight. According to researchers, for every two pounds of body weight we carry, we require just one gram of protein to maintain it. If we train hard enough and stimulate muscle growth, we will require a little extra protein,

along with additional carbohydrates and fats, to allow for that growth to take place. So, if you weigh 200 pounds, you will need 100 grams of protein per day to maintain your existing mass. If you are one of those above-average bodybuilders who find it easy to gain ten pounds of muscle a year, remember that you'll still need only 6,000 extra calories in a year over what you'll need for energy. Broken down to a daily figure as described earlier, that's only about 16 extra calories a day. Since one gram of protein contains 4 calories, a gram of fat contains 9 calories, and a gram of carbohydrate contains 4 calories, you would actually require only 4 grams of protein a day above your maintenance needs, which is less than the protein contained in one egg.

Most of the champion bodybuilders I know who are trying to increase their size and strength have been consuming anywhere from 250 to 400 grams of protein a day. That's far more than any nutritional scientist would recommend for muscle-building purposes.

Translating it into actual numbers just proves that you don't need as many calories or nearly as much protein as you might have been led to believe. Just as most bodybuilders have been seduced by the overly simplistic and erroneous notion that if a little training is good, then three times as much is that much more productive, they also seem to have been taken in by this mistaken belief with regard to their diet. They figure, if 100 grams of protein is required to help the body build muscle, then 300 grams "must" build muscle three times faster. This just isn't so. In fact, excess protein above what is needed for repair and possible growth can turn to fat just as readily as calories derived from excess quantities of carbohydrates and fats will.

Whenever you do eat protein, it should be of top quality so that your body's needs will be fully realized. If you're relying solely on regular foods for your protein needs, you should concentrate on animal proteins such as poultry, eggs, beef, and fish, which yield good-quality protein that your body can effectively use.

NUTRITIONAL CONSIDERATIONS FOR BECOMING LEAN

If you've been gorging yourself with protein and excess calories, you likely have been finding it difficult to improve or even maintain your muscular definition. The first thing you should do is figure out what number of calories you need to maintain your current weight. (Many health facilities and retailers offer charts that list calorie needs according to weight.) Then, if you want to lose weight and increase your muscular definition, eat less.

Once you've burned up 3,500 more calories than you require to maintain your current weight, you'll lose a pound of fat. Burn up 7,000 calories and you'll lose two pounds, and so on. If you have adequate

muscular definition already and just want to increase your muscle mass—something for which all reasonable bodybuilders should strive—then eat only a few extra calories above your energy needs. The same with protein: eat just a little extra to allow for the muscle growth you have stimulated to take place. All of this is easy to accept if you keep in mind that most bodybuilders won't gain even ten pounds of muscle a year; you shouldn't expect to see weight gains every time you step on a scale either. Muscle growth is a relatively slow process, and overeating won't hasten it along.

Overeating just builds fat—not muscle—something you should make every effort to avoid.

A former bodybuilding champion of my acquaintance has been quoted as saying that diet is responsible for 75 percent of a bodybuilder's success. With all due respect to the physique champion, I must say that he was spreading it a bit thick with that one. A bodybuilder can follow the world's most perfect diet, and if his training is deficient, he will never make the gains he could be making. The reverse, however, is not true; muscle has been shown to grow even on a starvation diet—*if* the training stimulation is of sufficient intensity. Diet is incredibly simple as long as a reasonable effort is made to eat well-balanced meals. Be a bodybuilder—not a health food or supplement fanatic. They're two separate animals.

17

Common Training Mistakes to Avoid

The world of body-building—and athletic training in general—is rife with ritual, myth, and nonsense. My wife, Terri, and I own a personal training facility, Nautilus North Strength & Fitness Centre, in which we train individuals on a one-on-one basis. We, along with my brother-in-law and master trainer Cary Howe, have personally supervised in excess of forty-one thousand of these one-on-one workouts.

As we review the records of each client's sessions, patterns emerge with regard to the impact of higher and lower sets, greater and lesser degrees of intensity, and optimal training frequency. In addition, having such close contact with our clients means that we discuss all manner of topics with them, and training and diet are foremost on the list. We have been asked hundreds of questions about the training fad du jour and the latest nutritional supplement. In almost every case, the revolutionary new training method and the miraculous nutritional breakthrough are neither revolutionary nor miraculous. They typically represent a quantum leap in the opposite direction from what the realm of science and what our own empirical observations have reported.

Most people look to us as "experts" and value our opinions by virtue of the fact that we own a fitness center, or they assume that my views on exercise, diet, and bodybuilding "must" have merit because they have been published. In many cases the clients' attitude is "You're the expert; you tell me what to do." They don't want reasons or evidence, but simply orders.

This is an appalling situation. Being a species that survives by the employment of our faculty of reason, we should operate only on the principle of having at least one valid reason for doing whatever it is we are doing. One's health, moreover, should be considered paramount, and to readily hand over one's volition and health to a gym owner or published author—with no further justification for doing so—qualifies as an "appeal to authority," an elemental fallacy in human cognition.

Against this backdrop, we insist on providing our clients with reasons for the prescriptions we offer at Nautilus North. We also provide data in the form of either independent studies or our own studies that support our contentions. It has been my experience that people who understand the principles and processes of what is involved to build their bodies are less likely to be frustrated in their efforts in the gym, and they are more motivated to engage in the process required to accomplish their objectives.

The main problem with appealing to experts is that there are many self-proclaimed "experts" in the field of bodybuilding who are misinformed and who delight in misleading inexperienced bodybuilders in what they claim is the "right way" to train. In the hopes of providing you with some intellectual ammunition to take with you on future visits to the gym, I offer the following roundup of some of the training aberrations that take place daily in most gymnasiums throughout North America.

IGNORING THE GENETIC FACTOR

One's bodybuilding success, as with most other things in athletics, is largely determined by one's genetic endowment. Training can augment genetics if it is proper training, but the training by itself will not turn a nonathlete into a world champion.

I happen to reside in Canada, where hockey is the national pastime. In the world of hockey, the three biggest names to emerge in the past thirty years are Gordie Howe, Bobby Orr, and Wayne Gretzky. Essentially all of the hockey players from thirty years ago trained the way Gordie Howe did, all of the players from twenty years ago trained the way Bobby Orr did, and most of the players of the past ten years train as Wayne Gretzky did. If the way these three stars trained were directly responsible for the stellar success they enjoyed in the sport, then there would currently be tens of thousands of athletes enjoying identical success and fame. The reality is that after thirty years, there remain only Howe, Orr, and Gretzky at the top of the hill. The reason? Genetics.

Similarly in bodybuilding, certain individuals are born with superior genetics for building larger-than-average muscles. These genetic factors include muscle length, as a muscle's width will never exceed its length; bone size, as bones that are too frail will not support a heavy musculature; myostatin levels—the higher the concentration of this protein in one's system, the less muscle one will be able to develop; and, perhaps most significant, the degree of muscle fiber density—that is, the number of muscle fibers in a given inch of a muscle's cross-sectional area.

For instance, I may have four hundred thousand muscle fibers in my biceps. Arnold Schwarzenegger, by contrast, may have eight hundred thousand fibers in his biceps. If both of us were to develop our biceps to be twice as strong and thick in size, his arms would still be twice the size of mine—and there isn't anything I can do to improve the situation. To compound the irony, if I followed the most scientific training program in the world and were able to effectively double the size of all of the existing fibers in my biceps, and Arnold followed a training program that was 50 percent less effective in stimulating the muscle fibers of his biceps, he would still have bigger biceps than mine, even though the size of my biceps muscles would have grown by 100 percent while his grew by only 50 percent.

This is why asking a genetically gifted athlete or bodybuilder for advice, or basing your workout on such advice, is almost always a mistake. These individuals have a genetic predisposition to be bigger and stronger than the average person long before they ever touch a weight. Given the natural proclivity of our species to conserve energy, these gifted athletes typically employ a less demanding approach to training—featuring lots of sets and lower intensity—because they can get away with it, owing to their genetics, and still make some progress. On their already advanced physiques, that relatively modest progress will always look more impressive than substantial progress on a physique that does not possess the same genetic gifts.

CHRONIC OVERTRAINING

Overtraining is one of the most significant contributors to the decline of muscular progress in the average trainee. Leaving the world of conventional training myths aside for a moment, the facts of the training situation are as follows: A muscle can be fully stimulated to hypertrophy, or grow; this can be accomplished with as little as one or two sets per bodypart. However, once growth stimulation has been induced, the muscles require many hours to recover and grow. Depending on the strength of the individual, two weeks or even more could be required for complete recovery and growth to occur.

If training is resumed before recovery has taken place, a loss of muscular size and strength will follow; if training is resumed before growth has taken place, no progress will follow; and if too much time is allowed to elapse between workouts, the muscles will atrophy, or shrink. Therefore, any program recommending that you train without sufficient time allocated for full recovery and growth between workouts is going to be nonproductive at best and counterproductive at worst.

People with absolutely zero training experience are best advised to train no more than three days per week (e.g., Monday, Wednesday, and Friday), with no more than two sets per bodypart. In time, the trainee should be able to reduce the number of sets to one, and the weekly workouts to one as well. Anyone who tells you otherwise is misinformed about the requisites of muscular hypertrophy.

LACK OF CONSISTENCY

The most common excuse for missing bodybuilding workouts is the perennial "I don't have time." While this protestation should certainly be true of someone facing the prospect of marathon or six-day-per-week training, it certainly should never apply to proper training for muscular mass and strength increases, which, at the most, should take a mere twenty to forty-five minutes per workout once to three times per week. In fact, in a recent experiment a subject noted dramatic muscular growth on a program of one two-minute workout repeated every two weeks!

Again, the name of the game in terms of continuing size and strength increases is intensity of effort. The harder you engage in an activity required to solicit an adaptive response of overcompensation (muscle growth), the less time you can engage in the activity. This simple law of physics regarding intensity and duration is not subject to anyone's suspect opinion—no matter how big the person's muscles or pocketbook.

If muscular progress can be observed with a time investment of a meager forty-five minutes per week, how can anyone justify the "don't have time" argument, short of a major emotional crisis? If you have fifteen minutes three times a week to read a book, talk on the telephone, watch TV, or eat more food, then you unquestionably have enough time to stimulate some muscular growth via exercise. If the bitter truth is that you flat-out have no inclination to exercise, then admit it and be prepared to accept the consequences of that stance.

POOR FORM

Most trainees have a tendency to want to impress whoever happens to be within a hundred yards of them, so they select heavy weights that they think will make people take notice, as opposed to weights that will thoroughly stimulate the muscles to get bigger and stronger, which, presumably, is the reason they originally joined the gym.

Once a force other than muscular contraction is made to do the work, how is the muscle group in question going to receive any stimulation? Using a weight that is so heavy that you have to heave it up actually involves only the barest minimum of muscle fibers required to move the resistance. Your objective as a bodybuilder is to involve as many fibers as possible to ensure maximum muscle stimulation and thereby broaden your chances of muscular hypertrophy. Fast or momentum-based repetitions should be avoided due to their inefficiency and also their potential for injury.

A properly performed repetition should take eight seconds: two seconds to raise the resistance, another two seconds in the position of full muscular contraction, and then four seconds—twice as long as it took you to raise the weight—to lower the resistance back to the starting position. All in all, it should take you exactly sixty-four seconds to complete a properly performed set of eight repetitions.

ARBITRARILY TERMINATING A SET

Many bodybuilders terminate a set simply because they start to feel uncomfortable, or else they stop when they hit a preconceived number of repetitions. Both of these approaches are wrong owing to the fact that in each case the bodybuilder never reaches positive failure.

A muscle has three levels of strength: a positive level (the weakest), which is exhausted whenever you are unable to lift the resistance for a complete repetition; a static level (the second strongest), which is exhausted whenever you are unable to hold a weight at any point throughout a given muscle's range of motion; and a negative level (the strongest level), which is exhausted whenever you are unable to lower the resistance from a position of full contraction to a position of full extension under deliberate, conscious control.

You cannot cause an adaptive response from your body by the mere performance of that which is already well within the body's existing capabilities. It can already handle such a demand without the need of overcompensation in the form of bigger and stronger muscles. Muscle growth must literally be forced; a demand must be placed on the body signaling that the existing levels of muscular size are inadequate for dealing with the stressors to which they are being exposed in the form of high-intensity exercise.

The greater the intensity of the exercise, the greater the corresponding need for muscular overcompensation. Also, the greater the intensity of exercise, the briefer the body's needed exposure to it. With these facts having now been presented to you, you can see that any exercise performed that stops short of (at least) positive failure is unproductive and, simply stated, a waste of time.

To force growth, your muscles must be called upon to attempt the momentarily impossible, to continue contracting until no further movement is possible. These last seemingly impossible and brutally hard repetitions of a set are solely responsible for stimulating the adaptive response from the central nervous system. The antecedent repetitions merely warm up the stressed muscle group in preparation for the effort required to attempt that last repetition.

IMPROPER STRUCTURING

Although more and more bodybuilders are beginning to train intelligently in that they are training no more than one to three days per week, the vast majority of these trainees construct routines that employ exercises in the wrong sequence. It is common to see bodybuilders start with their calves or arms and finish up by training their legs.

Unless specializing, this is incorrect from the physiological standpoint of localized reserves that are used up in proportion to the stressor that taps them. If you train your arms, chest, back, shoulders, and calves as hard as is required to stimulate growth, then it is highly unlikely that you will retain sufficient energy, as well as inclination, to train your legs as hard as is required to stimulate growth in them. Your legs, having the largest and most powerful muscles in the body, naturally require the most energy when trained properly in high-intensity style. It also stands to reason that you will have more energy to expend on them at the beginning of your workout while you are still fresh and your reserves are as yet untapped.

Your other muscle groups require less energy to be trained properly, owing to their comparatively smaller size and strength. They should be trained in descending order of their amplitude after you have trained your legs.

The ideal structuring of a routine intended to stimulate maximum muscle growth in all major muscle groups would be as follows:

1. Legs
2. Back
3. Chest
4. Shoulders
5. Arms

With this sequence, you can be confident that the muscle groups that require the most energy are able to receive it when their energy reserves are at their fullest and, consequently, when the most energy is readily available.

HIGH REPS FOR ABS

Go into a typical gym these days and you're sure to notice at least two or three individuals grinding out set after set of high-repetition exercises for their abdominal muscles in the mistaken hope that they will somehow "develop" their abs.

The abdominals are composed of skeletal muscle, just like the biceps, triceps, chest,

Your abdominal muscles are skeletal muscles, and—as with all skeletal muscle—they respond best to intense, brief, and infrequent training.

train your midsection with weights because it will make your waist bigger. Instead, you should perform endless sets of sit-ups without resistance (and I know of trainees who employ 2,000 repetitions per day in this exercise) to develop your midsection without increasing its size." I ask you: how can you "develop" any muscle group without increasing its size? If this is a legitimate phenomenon, what then could the word *develop* possibly denote? If you train to develop your muscles, then something about their existing condition must change for the better—that is, they must get stronger. The stronger a muscle gets, the bigger it gets. This is elementary physiology. Therefore, any attempt to develop a particular muscle group, if successful, must result in an increase in that muscle group's size and strength. It follows that you should train your abs as you would any other skeletal muscle group: with weights.

BULKING UP

Although bulking up is not as much in vogue as it used to be, there are still misguided bodybuilders who equate muscle size with body weight increases. Consequently, they overeat in an attempt to "grow" muscles. If muscles could be made to hypertrophy merely by the consumption of food, there would be no need to ever go to the gym, and Orson Welles would have been the most muscular man on earth.

Obviously, it is stimulation via exercise that causes a muscle to hypertrophy,

lats, deltoids, quads, and so forth, and they respond best to exercises that involve their contracting against resistance. You wouldn't expect to develop your biceps by performing endless sets and reps of curls with no weight in your hands. Likewise, don't expect to notice any significant results by training your abs with an infinite variety of sets and reps of sit-ups, leg raises, and the like, sans resistance. Train your abs as you would any other muscle group, and they will respond in like manner via the overcompensation process. Then rely on a reduced-calorie diet to provide the definition required.

Don't be taken in by the frequently repeated lore that instructs: "You shouldn't or increase in size. While nutrition plays a role in the overcompensation process, it is a minor one. Force-feeding yourself excessive calories will result only in covering up whatever muscular development you have attained under a blanket of adiposity. If you're a competitive bodybuilder, that blanket will have to be shed through severe dieting. Nine times out of ten, that dieting leads to a loss of muscle mass in addition to the fat stores. Furthermore, it has been established that once you create fat cells by overeating, they will never leave the body, but only reduce in size.

Therefore, allowing yourself to acquire additional bodyfat is never in your best interest (save for sumo wrestling). It not only detracts from your physique but also will have to be shed via overtraining and undereating before a contest. Neither of these remedies leads to the development of muscle mass or is conducive to winning physique contests. The next time someone tells you to "drink on those muscular gains" from a food supplement or engineered food, recognize that the directive is a testament to that person's ignorance of both nutritional and physiological reality.

INCORRECT HAND PLACEMENT

Almost every bodybuilder mistakenly believes that a wide grip gives you more stretch than a close grip. In fact, it gives you less stretch, in terms of range of motion.

This phenomenon was best explained by Mike Mentzer, who said, "If you can

Wide-grip pull-down. When you use a wide grip, the attachment point of the latissimus muscle under the arm comes into close proximity to the other lat attachment lower down on the back, thus reducing the range through which the latissimus muscle must move during a repetition.

picture a muscle as a rubber band stretched between two points, the origin and insertion of the muscle, it stands to reason that the muscle will be stretched the most and forced to contract over a greater range of motion when those two attachment points are the greatest distance apart from each other. By performing wide-grip exercises like chins, you can see that the attachment of the lat under the arm comes into close proximity to the other lat attachment lower down on the back. Therefore, the actual stretch has been

Close-grip pull-down. When the arms are closer together in this exercise, the latissimus muscle is stretched the most and thus made to contract over a greater range of motion.

activates many muscle fibers that would have remained unstressed had you opted to use a wide grip. Ergo, a close grip should be employed whenever a choice exists in the performance of an exercise. You will stimulate more muscle fibers and increase your range of motion and, hence, the productivity of the exercise.

HIGH REPS FOR DEFINITION

Bodybuilders who still believe in the myths of previous generations unquestioningly accept as true the contention that the more sets and reps you do, the more definition you get. The implication here is that bodybuilding, per se, utilizes fat cells as fuel, and so, the more you perform a particular activity, the leaner you will become. Unfortunately, even with highly repetitive tasks such as running, the reality is that you would have to engage in the activity for up to eleven hours straight in order to burn off one pound of bodyfat. Moreover, in order to perform a high volume of any activity, it would have to be of such a low intensity that it would do nothing to increase your lean body mass.

After all, if your muscles become accustomed to doing low-intensity work, there would be no biological reason for your body to build (or even preserve) a muscle mass that was developed to handle heavy weights in a high-intensity fashion. As a consequence, the body will reduce its level of muscle mass in proportion to the effort those muscles are made to exert on a routine

reduced. On the other hand, when the hand spacing is close together directly overhead, you can see that the two points of attachment are farther apart and thus there is a much greater stretch involved."

This is true of most of the exercises involving the larger muscles of the torso—including chins, incline and supine bench presses, and lat machine pull-downs. You will obtain superior results from these exercises when you perform them properly—over a full range of motion. This approach basis. And as far as "burning bodyfat" goes, bodybuilding burns carbohydrates, which it has converted to glycogen, or blood sugar—not fats—as its preferred fuel for intense muscular contractions.

Since high intensity and long duration are on opposite ends of the spectrum in terms of their metabolic costs, increasing your sets and/or reps means that you are decreasing your training intensity. Further, since intensity must be maintained in order for your body to either build muscle mass or hold on to its existing levels, all that the lowering of intensity will yield is a loss of muscle tissue.

While it's true that the repetitive performance of any activity will result in the utilization of calories for energy, it does not follow that the performance of any activity is the most efficacious way to shed bodyfat. Granted, activities such as walking, jogging, cycling, and swimming will burn calories that can contribute to one's fat-loss program. However, one will burn more calories by building more muscle tissue, because bigger muscles burn more calories 24-7, as opposed to burning calories only during the time you are working out. Think of it this way: just as it requires more energy to heat a bigger room than a smaller room, it takes more energy (calories) to sustain a bigger muscle than it does to sustain a smaller one.

Thus, it behooves trainees looking to become leaner to build as much muscle as they can hold and then let the higher metabolic rate that comes with bigger muscles

work for their fat-burning interests. That course is far superior to engaging in low-intensity activity that not only doesn't burn much in the way of calories (you would have to run for thirty-five miles to burn one pound of fat) but also can actually reduce the size of the muscles owing to the lower muscular output required to perform them.

The key, then, is to continue to build muscle up, while simultaneously reducing your calorie intake below your maintenance level to use up the body's fat stores for fuel and rid your physique of the bête noire of adiposity. Remember that muscle is what gives members of either sex their distinctive and appealing shape. Fat itself is formless.

EXCESSIVE SETS

Performing excessive sets is a mistake for two reasons: it can cause you to fail at a point of cardiovascular fatigue, as opposed to muscular failure; and it withholds you from going to true positive failure in any of the exercises in anticipation of the exercise to follow. By the time you get to your sixth, seventh, eighth, or ninth exercise (depending on how many repetitions you performed during your prior sets), you likely will be breathing like a racehorse, and your oxygen debt will be such that you're forced to use very light weights, which do little to stimulate an adaptive response from the body.

Unless the goal of the training is specialization or purely to obtain some cardiovascular benefit, there is no reason for any trainee to perform more than one or two sets for any bodypart. The central principle when training is to work each muscle group to a state of legitimate muscular failure.

This is only a sample of the errors that are being made in bodybuilding gymnasiums around the world. If you have been guilty of committing any of them, you no longer have any excuse for continuing down the wrong path. If in the future some ignorant gym rat tries to mislead you or some innocent newcomer to bodybuilding regarding any of these facts, you now have the wherewithal to set the record straight.

18

Questions and Answers

As a new trainee, you're bound to have questions. What follows are common questions I have received through seminars I have conducted at my training facility, followed by my responses.

IMMEDIATE GAINS

QUESTION: I have been training for just under one year, and I must say that I am very disappointed with my lack of results. The reason I undertook weight training was to get bigger, and yet in the past months I haven't added a single pound. My question to you is which exercises do you think I should be performing in order to best build muscle mass, and to build it quickly?

Answer:
As a rule, it is best to concentrate on the exercises that involve the largest muscle masses of the body, such as thighs, back,

and chest. For specific growth stimulation of these bodyparts, I recommend isolation movements such as leg extensions, pull-overs, and dumbbell flies. If, however, your goal is to build overall muscle mass, then I recommend compound movements, which tax many more muscle groups, stimulate many more muscle fibers overall, and produce greater accumulative muscle growth, although they will not stimulate certain muscle groups nearly as thoroughly as will the isolation movements. Examples of such compound movements are squats, bent-over rows or chin-ups, standing presses, bench presses, and parallel bar dips.

Even more important than the exercises you select is the manner in which you perform them. If you give each exercise everything you've got while maintaining proper form and using what for you is a heavy weight, then you will grow. That said, don't let blind ambition override metaphysical reality: don't expect to gain a pound of muscle a day or even a pound of pure muscle tissue a week. That degree of progress is beyond the physiological scope and metabolic pathways of nine-tenths of the people on this planet.

Proper diet is integral as well, in that it provides the nutrients necessary for growth, once you've stimulated the muscle with hard training. A well-balanced diet with a slight emphasis on increasing your carbohydrate and calorie intake should aid you in reaching the muscle size that you

desire—providing that you have assessed your genetic potential correctly.

EATING BREAD

QUESTION: You mentioned that it's all right for a person to eat anything he wants, and as long as his total calorie intake is reduced, he will lose bodyfat. I was wondering if this holds true for bread as well?

Answer:
Yes. Inasmuch as bread is a "thing," you can still eat any thing, inclusive of bread, that you want, and as long as your total calorie intake is reduced, you will lose bodyfat. There is nothing fattening about bread, per se; a slice of enriched white bread contains only seventy calories.

Likewise, don't be deterred by the maxim that warns, "It's not the bread that is fattening; it's what you put on it." It is, rather, the total number of calories consumed above your personal maintenance need in the course of a day—or accumulatively throughout a week, month, or year—that results in the acquisition and/or expansion of adipose tissue. Bread, jams, peanut butter, margarine, and the like are not of themselves going to cause you to become fat. Now, if you were to consume your maintenance need of calories and then have bread and/or spread, the calories in that added snack could prove to be the proverbial straw that broke the camel's back and cause you to gain some bodyfat. Even then, though, you would have to eat approximately twenty-five slices of bread and peanut butter over and above your daily maintenance need of calories to gain one pound of fat.

So, bread itself is safe to consume while dieting. In his book The Nautilus Nutrition Book (Contemporary Books, 1981), Ellington Darden, Ph.D., recounted how Michigan State University conducted a nutritional study in which college students who were allowed to eat what-ever they wanted—provided they ate twelve slices of high-fiber bread each day—lost weight. The bread was filling, so it curbed their desire for additional food, and it was comparatively low in calories, which would account for the weight loss, providing their total calorie intake was below their maintenance need of calories. Bon appétit.

THE NEED FOR A WEIGHT BELT

QUESTION: Do I need a weight belt or not? I just recently started training and noticed that while some bodybuilders wear them, others never do. Are they a necessity, or simply a custom?

Answer:
The answer depends solely upon your choice of exercises. If you routinely engage in exercises that, from a kinesiology stand-point, are potentially or actually stressful to your vertebrae, then yes, you should wear a lifting belt. Exercises such as standing presses, dead lifts, squats, and barbell (and particularly T-bar) rowing put major pressure not only on your erector spinae muscles but also on your spine. While a belt does not prevent pressure from being directed toward your lower back, it does aid in the dissipation and distribution of the pressure. That benefit will definitely prolong your training life and help stave off the possibility of injury.

Technically, belts are required only for free-weight movements. Machines such as Max Contraction, Nautilus, Universal, and Kaiser are kinesthetically designed and manufactured to eliminate the mechanical drawbacks of free weights. Even so, your observation that some body-builders wear belts, while others don't, is an accurate description of the general state of affairs. Some wear them for legiti-mate reasons, such as for performing heavy power lifts, in which they need all the support and protection they can get. Others, I suspect, are more "poseur" than serious bodybuilder. They wear lifting belts usually along with conspicuously torn T-shirts, lifting gloves (OOH!—now, there's a real necessity) and, of course, the obligatory leather straps—for "support purposes"! Then, all decked out in this gear and resembling a cross between Marlon Brando in The Wild One and a knight from the Middle Ages, they walk over to a moderately weighted barbell, draw and expel several loud breaths, and proceed to throw the weight up and down *in a remote attempt to perform a set of barbell curls, all the while screaming like a banshee. This is palpable nonsense to those who know anything about the requisites of productive exercise, and it is needlessly off-putting to newcomers to the science.*

In summary, if you are going to seriously perform a heavy set of standing presses, barbell or T-bar rows, dead lifts, or squats, or if you are experiencing back problems, then a belt would be a useful item to have among your training paraphernalia. If, however, you're thinking of purchasing a belt because other people are wearing them, then stop now before you digress to the point where you've become one of the attention-seeking masters of interruption just described.

Look for valid reasons why you should or should not obtain or pursue something; don't look to convention. In the quest for training truth, there can be no sacred cows. Tradition, convention, imitation, and custom have no place in the training concepts of the modern bodybuilder. Only facts should anchor your premises, your conclusions, and, in the end, your actions—not only in your training but also in all other aspects of your life.

HEAVY BARBELL CURLS—THE GREATEST MASS BUILDER?

QUESTION: My bodybuilding instructor at the gym tells me that in order to build my arms, I must perform barbell curls, because heavy weights can be employed, and they are "the greatest mass builder for the biceps." However, whenever I perform them, I don't really feel the movement to be that much more effective than any other curling movement that I have done for my biceps. Should I stick with them regardless, due to his having more experience than I in such matters, or should I change the exercise for another biceps movement?

Answer:

Thank you for exposing perhaps the biggest fraud in bodybuilding today: the myth that heavy barbell curls are somehow superior to any other type of curling exercise for strengthening and overdeveloping the biceps. Barbell curls—though a good exercise—are not "the greatest mass builder for the biceps." They work the biceps predominantly in the muscles' weakest range of motion; there is no resistance in the starting position of the movement, nor is there any resistance at the top—or finish—of the movement, the most important part. So, of the three areas throughout the range of the movement in which the muscle fibers of the biceps could be stimulated—the bottom, the middle, and the top—the biceps receive thorough stimulation in only one portion, the middle.

Any exercise that stimulates fibers primarily in the weakest range of a muscle can hardly be said to be the best. To claim that it is "the greatest" exercise for the biceps in terms of productivity is ludicrous.

To activate more muscle fibers, which, in turn, stimulates more growth, an exercise should contain resistance in the fully contracted position. Ergo, the biceps muscles will be best stimulated by exercises that meet this strongest-range criterion. That list includes concentration curls, steep-angle Scott or preacher bench curls, any form of cable curls, chin-ups, and Max Contraction machine, Nautilus machine, or Hammer Strength machine curls. All of these exercises provide resistance to the biceps in their strongest range of motion and consequently stimulate many more of the fibers of the biceps muscle than does the inefficient old standard, the barbell curl.

The fact that heavier weights can be employed in movements such as the barbell curl isn't really germane, owing to the fact that other muscle groups assist in the lift (e.g., the lower back, rectus abdominus, serratus, anterior deltoid, legs, forearms, and trapezius). The effect is that even the little stimulation that the biceps receive during the movement is compromised and dissipated through the involvement of the assisting muscle groups.

Returning to your question, then: go ahead and substitute another biceps exercise for barbell curls. The only additional "mass" that barbell curls contribute to building is the massive wedge of ignorance that separates bodybuilders from objective physiological fact.

MUSCLE STRETCHING

QUESTION: Is it possible, as some bodybuilders and massage therapists contend, to actually stretch or lengthen a muscle by performing exercises that excessively stretch it? I have a girlfriend who takes Pilates and claims that she is lengthening her muscles with the resistance exercises her instructor prescribes. Moreover, an instructor at my gym says that it is possible to extend a short biceps by performing Scott curls and that a small calf muscle can be made into a full one by the performance of standing calf raises. If so, how is this process accomplished?

Answer:

To my knowledge, it is not possible to lengthen muscles to any appreciable degree by stretching them. Our muscles are attached to our bones via tendons, so the only way they could be "lengthened" would be to have the tendons surgically cut and then reattached further down the bone. Such a procedure is neither pleasurable nor practical. Full-range Scott curls, or preacher curls, do serve to stretch the biceps muscle but do little or nothing to alter the length of this muscle group.

For example, witness the biceps of former Mr. Olympia winners Chris Dickerson and Franco Columbu. These are men who performed preacher curls frequently and extensively over the course of their competitive bodybuilding careers, yet they never acquired the long, full biceps of the exercise's namesake, Larry Scott. Their biceps remained short, though impressive in their own right.

Muscle length is a genetic trait and, as such, is not subject to alteration, shy of surgery. Don't worry about the fact that your biceps are not as full as Mike Mentzer's or as highly peaked as Robby Robinson's, because these traits are genetically predetermined. Just as we can't all be over six feet tall and have the face of Brad Pitt, neither can we all be genetically gifted in the physique department like Arnold Schwarzenegger.

Simply train hard and develop yourself to the best of your genetic potential. You cannot accurately compare yourself or your achievements against the accomplishments of anybody but yourself. Similarly, owing to innate physiological differences, other people, including bodybuilding champions, cannot accurately compare themselves with you. You're unique, and it is always infinitely more desirable to cultivate your specific individuality to its fullest potential rather than to copy someone who has done likewise. Who knows? Your genetic potential, once realized through intelligent training and dietary principles, may far exceed that of the champions—but you'll never realize that potential unless you try.

"STABILIZER" MUSCLES

QUESTION: I've heard that using machines rather than free weights will prevent me from developing stabilizer muscles that help control movement. What's a stabilizer muscle?

Answer:

Many people seem to believe that there is a classification of muscles known as "stabilizer muscles." No anatomy book supports that assumption. That's because there are only three classifications of muscles in human beings: smooth, cardiac, and skeletal. Skeletal muscles, when strengthened, not only are able to contract more forcefully but also can stabilize various bodyparts when called upon to do so.

If you ask a "stabilizer muscle" proponent what stabilizer muscles are, the likely reply is that they simply "exist" on either side of joints, but this doesn't mean there are little bands of "stabilizer" muscles that come into play whenever you're lifting free weights but that remain dormant if you use an exercise machine. During the performance of a free-weight bench press, for instance, the barbell isn't pressed in a zigzag or elliptical fashion; instead, a certain "groove" is found—a straight up-and-down motion—and the trainee proceeds to perform the exercise in this fashion. Performing it in any other fashion would be dangerous. This exercise requires the involvement of many muscle groups—all of which can be located in an anatomy book—such as the anterior deltoid, the triceps, the pectorals, the lats, the abdominals, and even the legs to some degree. Remember that all skeletal muscles contract by shortening, producing movement. In exercises such as the bench press, that action results in the arms moving in a linear fashion—not from side to side. There would be no effective stability if this were reversed.

The argument in favor of "stabilizer" muscles came about due to the influence of manufacturers of free weights who saw their market threatened by the influx of training machines such as Nautilus in the early 1980s. It was at this point that one first heard of the need for "stabilizer" muscle development and the contention that only free weights afforded the trainee that opportunity.

The truth is that a stronger muscle is better able to stabilize, or secure, the joint it surrounds. For example, the quadriceps and hamstring muscles help stabilize the knee joint; the stronger the muscle, the stronger the tendons and the more stable the joint. A leg extension machine and leg curl machine will strengthen these muscles and their tendons just as effectively as any free-weight exercise, if not more effectively. So, the leg extension and leg curl exercise are indeed effective in developing stability in the knee area. And so on with every other muscle group.

The primary muscles involved in stability directly affect the trunk: namely, the rectus abdominus and the erector spinae muscles of the lower back. Here again, performing a set of crunches on an abdominal

machine and a set on a Nautilus or MedX lower back machine will strengthen these important muscles. Among other functions, they provide stability to the trunk during exercise.

BODYBUILDING AND CARDIO

QUESTION: I have a question regarding cardiovascular fitness and bodybuilding's ability to provide it. Having just finished rereading Dr. Kenneth Cooper's fine book, *Aerobics* (Bantam, 1968), I'm rather doubtful about weight training's ability to provide for cardiovascular fitness. In fact, in the second chapter he states that "a body beautiful, and not much more" is about all you can expect to get from strength training. He then goes on to imply that strength training is no replacement for conventional cardio activities such as cycling, swimming, and running. What are your thoughts on this matter? Can strength training be utilized for cardio exercise by people like me, who, though respecting what men such as Dr. Cooper say, nevertheless are not overly fond of running? And how would the program differ from your conventional strength-training program, if at all?

Answer:
Thank you for giving me the opportunity to correct some serious flaws in the reasoning of Dr. Kenneth Cooper, which I'll attempt to address at some length in my reply. Bodybuilding, or "strength training,"

has been ignorantly maligned over the years, and one of the prime reasons for this ignorance is the bias of purported fitness "experts" like Dr. Cooper.

Not only is strength training capable of providing the cardiovascular fitness about which you are justly concerned (heart disease being a leading cause of death in North America and Europe), but properly conducted, can also improve other aspects of conditioning, which, all together, comprise total fitness.

Many individuals are of the impression that strength training is something divorced from the heart and lungs. It was never scratched in stone that human beings can get a cardiovascular training effect only from treadmills, ellipticals, Reebok step classes, and dance aerobics. In fact, it has been proven time and again scientifically that high-intensity strength-training exercise will stimulate the body to produce substantial and profound cardio-vascular adaptation—and many more fitness benefits besides that conventional low-intensity aerobic exercise cannot.

Of particular note is a study reported in Orlando, Florida, in 2004, at the conference of the World Organization of Family Doctors. The presenter, Erika Baum, M.D., stated that pure weight training can markedly improve aerobic fitness. She cited a six-month structured Nautilus strength-training program that "resulted in improvements in cardio-circulatory fitness to a degree traditionally considered obtainable only through endurance exercises such as running, bicycling, and swimming." According to Baum, a family physician at Philipps University, in Marburg, Germany, "This opens up new possibilities for cardio-pulmonary-oriented exercise besides the traditional stamina sports." New exercise options are desirable because some patients just don't care for endurance exercise, which doesn't do much to improve muscular strength and stabilization.

Baum reported on thirty-one healthy but physically unfit subjects aged twenty to forty-five, including eight women, who completed a Nautilus weight-training program involving two or three thirty- to forty-minute sessions per week for six months. Their aerobic capacity, assessed on a graded treadmill exercise test, improved by 33 percent over the course of six months. Meanwhile, mean body weight declined from 171.51 pounds to 149.25 pounds. Resting heart rate dropped from a baseline of 68.5 beats per minute to 65.6. Heart rate measured three minutes after cessation of a maximal exercise test declined from a baseline of 108.7 beats per minute to 103.1, with a larger decrease in women than men. This study clearly established that high-intensity strength training, performed properly, challenges the cardiovascular system more than enough to keep it healthy.

Another study conducted in 1985 by Dr. Stephen Messier and Mary Dill, of Wake Forest University, and published in the science journal Research Quarterly for Exercise and Sport (56: 345–51), is equally noteworthy. Researchers measured the aerobic conditioning benefits on thirty-six male college students who employed one of three training approaches: (1) strength training in high-intensity style on Nautilus equipment, (2) lifting free weights in the traditional style, and (3) a running program. All subjects trained three times per week for ten weeks. The findings showed that the Nautilus group, who trained in a high-intensity fashion, exhibited the same aerobic adaptations that the runners did. The real kicker here is that the running group trained 50 percent longer than the Nautilus group—thirty minutes per session, compared with twenty minutes per session—establishing empirically that running was less efficient at stimulating cardiovascular benefits than strength training performed in circuit sequence. Performing "aerobic" training 50 percent more did not result in 50 percent more cardiovascular benefit—or even 10 percent more; it resulted in "0" additional benefit.

More recently, scientists working at McMaster University, in Hamilton, Ontario, discovered that a two-minute workout (consisting of stationary cycling for four thirty-second intervals at high intensity, with a four-minute break between intervals) performed on alternate days three times a week, for a total weekly exercise time of six minutes, resulted in "a doubling of the subjects' aerobic endurance levels after two weeks." The lead researcher, Professor Martin Gibala, stated, "We thought the findings were startling because it suggests the overall volume of exercise people need to do is lower than what's recommended." Indeed, instead of working out for twenty minutes, three times a week (minimum)—the protocol that most personal trainers and exercise specialists have been recommending for decades—this study showed that as few as four total sets lasting no more than thirty seconds each sufficed not merely to improve human cardiovascular function, but to double it!

Future testing of this procedure might well conclude that one such session per week, and perhaps even one or two thirty-second intervals, will produce similar or better results. Given that your heart and lungs can't tell whether you are working at maximum intensity on a stationary bike, as in the study, or at a leg press (or a lat pull-down or a shoulder press, for that matter), such results would, by extension, be obtainable by doing a high-intensity strength training set, resting for up to four minutes, and performing another set—as outlined in this book—until four such sets had been completed.

In fact, it is my opinion that the cardiovascular training effect that can be obtained using resistance training is superior to that of any other type of exercise. There is also a growing amount of medical opinion to the effect that all of the *supposed cardiovascular benefit to be had from exercise is a result of the muscles' becoming stronger, so that the heart doesn't have to work as hard, resulting in a lower pulse rate during more strenuous activity.*

According to cardiologist Henry Solomon, M.D., from his book The Exercise Myth:

Most of the improvement in functional capacity due to exercise is not even directly related to the heart. It is due to an effect on the peripheral muscle cells whereby they more efficiently extract oxygen from the blood.

Bruce Charash, M.D., current head of cardiology at Lenox Hill Hospital, in New York City, agrees. From his book Heart Myths:

When patients participate in exercise programs, they often assume that their heart becomes stronger. This is not the case. Physical training results in a sense of well-being because of other effects. It improves the efficiency of the muscles. It improves the hormonal tone of the body. It improves the control of sugar in people with diabetes. However, exercise will not make the heart beat more strongly.

According to a study by Goldberg, Elliot, and Kuehl, at the Human Performance Laboratory (Division of General Medicine, *Oregon Health Sciences Services, Portland, Oregon, published in the* Journal of Applied Science Research *vol. 2, no. 3 [1988]: 42–45):*

Traditional, non-circuit weight training for both the athlete and the general population can be viewed as a method of reducing myocardial oxygen demand during usual daily activities. This cardio-protective benefit allows the individual to perform isometric exertion combined with dynamic work with lower cardiac oxygen requirements, and, thus, improvement in cardiovascular efficiency. Although standard methods of weight training and strength acquisition may not improve running, cardiovascular benefits do occur.

Doug McGuff, M.D., in his excellent online article "Health Related Issues" (ultimate-exercise.com), states:

Equally important in cardiovascular health are *peripheral adaptations.* These are adaptations that actually occur within the working muscles that have indirect benefit for the cardiovascular system. The reason a frail 80-year-old gets more winded climbing a flight of stairs is not necessarily because their cardiovascular system is weak; it may be more due to the fact that their muscles are weak. A muscle is divided into segments called motor units. A motor unit is a group of muscle fibers all supplied by one motor nerve. If a motor nerve sends a signal to a motor unit, all the fibers in a motor unit will contract with 100 percent effort. Let us say that it takes a hundred units of work to climb a flight of stairs. If our 80-year-old's motor units all contain one unit of strength, it will take 100 motor units to provide 100 units of strength to get up the stairs. The 80-year-old's heart will have to pump hard enough to support the working of 100 motor units. If, however, my motor units each have two units of strength, it will only take me 50 motor units to provide 100 units of strength. My heart will have to pump hard enough to support the working of 50 motor units. If, through proper strength training, I double my strength, then each motor unit will have four units of strength. At this level, I will only have to recruit 25 motor units. At this level of strength, my perceived effort is much lower. Now, there are other factors involved that make this example imperfect. Increasing muscle size means more weight may have to be carried, or the body's cooling efficiency will be slightly less. However, the general idea still holds true. Proper exercise not only stimulates central cardiovascular changes, it stimulates peripheral muscular changes, which allows you to do more work with less stress to the cardiovascular support system.

McGuff elaborates on this point in another essay, entitled "Paradigm Shift for Exercise" (ultimate-exercise.com):

Despite its profound effects on the cardiovascular system, resistance training still has its major impacts through peripheral adaptations, mainly in terms of increased muscle strength. We have all told our patients that just performing activities of daily life (walking, taking the stairs, yard work) can preserve our cardiovascular health. Unfortunately, the age-related loss of muscle (sarcopenia) can undermine our ability to carry out those activities. Resistance training can prevent and even reverse sarcopenia. [Rogers M. A., and W. J. Evans. "Changes in skeletal muscle with aging: effects of exercise training." *Exercise and Sport Sciences Reviews* 21 (1993): 65–102.] Furthermore, as a muscle becomes stronger, fewer motor units will have to be recruited to perform a given task, thus reducing the demand on the cardiovascular system. Clearly, the best kind of exercise is the kind that will tax the musculature the most; this will create a powerful cardiovascular stimulus, while producing hemodynamic changes that minimize the risk of cardiac ischemia and also produce the most profound peripheral changes in the form of muscle strengthening.

This would explain why a scientific study conducted at West Point Military Academy in 1975 revealed that a high-intensity strength-training program performed on Nautilus machines stimulated the body to produce outstanding cardiovascular benefits (measured by more than sixty different tests to determine aerobic fitness) from workouts lasting as little as eighteen minutes. In other words, high-intensity strength training has your aerobic bases covered.

It's now been documented that, to produce the most profound changes in cardiovascular endurance, exercise has to be intense and brief (as in the McMaster study). The question that logically arises is: how frequently should one train to allow such adaptive responses to take place in the cardiovascular system? The revolutionary study conducted at West Point may be taken as a guiding example of the benefits of once-a-week training. Arthur Jones, the creator of Nautilus machines and the man who trained many of the cadets in the West Point study, addresses this subject in his essay entitled "Maximizing Aerobic Potential":

Properly performed, which they seldom are, strength building exercises are not a "good" way to improve cardiovascular condition; they are, instead, by far the best way to improve cardiovascular condition. . . . you move almost immediately from the end of the first exercise to the start of the second exercise, with almost no rest between the two exercises, then you will increase both strength and cardiovascular condition; in fact, that style of training, properly performed, will lead to a level of cardiovascular condition that is far higher than you could ever produce by any amount of jogging or any other cardiovascular exercise. Such a style of exercise simultaneously provides anaerobic exercise for strength building and aerobic exercise for improving cardiovascular condition. . . . Once you reach the *target* rate of exercise you will *find* that your pulse rate remains at a very high rate throughout the workout, far higher than you could ever maintain with any sort of aerobic exercise; yet your muscles are being worked anaerobically, as they must for strength-building purposes. . . . We used this style of training during research conducted at the United States Military Academy, West Point, twenty-two years ago, and the results were so outstanding that Dr. Kenneth Cooper refused to believe them, refused even though his own people performed all of the *pre* and post testing. Average strength for the *test* group increased by 60 percent in six weeks, while their cardiovascular condition reached a level so high that Cooper refused to believe it, a level he could not reach in six years of aerobic exercise . . . *producing the best possible results requires such a style of training no more than once a week. During the research at West Point, we trained the cadet subjects three times each week but used this "no rest" style of training only once each week.*

I hope this explanation will put to rest some of the baseless "anti-strength training" bias against bodybuilding exercise and its effect on our cardiovascular system that has posed as gospel truth within the bodybuilding and fitness industry.

"DEFINITION" EXERCISES

QUESTION: I have been bodybuilding for several years now and have made considerable gains in size and strength. It has struck me that perhaps, at this stage of my training, it would be wise for me to become ripped—but I still want to hold on to my existing size. What are the best definition exercises for the different bodyparts, in your opinion?

Answer:
First, let's be clear that there is no such thing as a "definition exercise." Definition, per se, is strictly a matter of shedding enough adipose (or, as it is more commonly known, fat) from under the skin in order to reveal the muscle in bold relief.

Because definition is exclusively a matter of losing fat, it is solely achieved through a combination of diet—taking in fewer calories than you expend—and activity levels. The bad news is that, even by fasting, you would be hard pressed to lose more than five or six ounces of fat per day, and while you will lose fat more quickly by markedly increasing your activity levels, the difference is not all that significant. The good news is that, while there is no such thing as a definition exercise, certain exercises require more energy than others, thus burning more calories, the excess of which is responsible for fat storage. Thus, they help in developing a more defined appearance.

Several self-styled authorities claim that leg extensions will specifically lead to the creation of thigh definition. Their logic eludes me. I don't comprehend how leg extensions are capable of "creating" thigh definition more quickly than, say, leg presses or squats. As a matter of fact, squats would probably be the best for creating "definition," in that they demand the greatest energy (i.e., calorie) expenditure.

The secret, then, to obtaining a more defined, or "ripped," appearance is to follow a calorie-reduced diet and select exercises that demand the most energy, such as squats or leg presses. In this way, not only are more calories burned, but also you will continue to stimulate muscle growth via the exercises themselves, provided you perform them with high intensity; larger muscles require and expend more calories at rest than does fat tissue. Your double dividend of training, when married to a reduced-calorie diet, gives you an unsurpassed three-pronged attack against the definition-obscuring demon of adiposity.

AMINO ACIDS

QUESTION: How many amino acids should one take for the purpose of building a muscularly massive physique?

Answer:

Your question implies that you accept the notion that amino acids are somehow a primary requisite in the development of "massive" muscles. They're not. This issue can be traced back a decade or so, when protein supplements became temporarily unpopular within the Food and Drug Administration, owing to the bogus claims made by overzealous manufacturers.

In an attempt to recapture the tremendously lucrative protein market, protein manufacturers reissued their protein supplements with a new name: "amino acids." It is a prime example of old wine in new skins. Amino acids are simply the

nitrogen-based constituents of protein and consequently are equally as ineffective in "building" muscle as their soy, milk, egg, and whey predecessors. Of course, the supplement makers changed not only their labels but also their marketing strategies: they began to promote a "new" product called "amino acids." In fact, their advertisements contained banner headlines proclaiming that they were actually safe, effective, and even superior replacements to anabolic steroids, which is tantamount to telling a man who is testosterone deficient that all he needs is a protein shake in order to rectify his hormonal imbalance.

Amino acid supplements are not a requisite for building big muscles. To build a larger-than-normal amount of muscle mass, you must first stimulate muscle growth at the cellular level via high-intensity training and then allow sufficient time to elapse between workouts for your muscular reserves to recover and for the growth that you have stimulated to manifest. Only then does nutrition become a factor in the growth process.

Adequate nutrition—including all nutrients and not just protein—must be provided in order for you to maintain your existing level of muscle mass. If you stimulated growth by training intensely enough, a little bit extra (approximately sixteen calories) must be consumed to, again, allow that growth to manifest.

A well-balanced diet comprising two or more (depending on body weight) portions of the four basic food groups (i.e., cereals and grains, fruits and vegetables, dairy products, and meats) consumed each day will provide you with sufficient nutrition to both maintain your health and, if you've stimulated it, allow for the growth of massive muscles. However, there is no way that amino acid supplements can of themselves either stimulate or enhance the muscle growth process. Caveat emptor!

To build bigger and stronger muscles, you must first stimulate muscle growth at the cellular level via high-intensity training and then allow sufficient time to elapse between workouts for your muscles to recover and grow.

Index

About the Author

For more than twenty years, John Little has worked alongside the sport's greatest champions and innovators—from Steve "Hercules" Reeves, Lou Ferrigno, and Arnold Schwarzenegger to six-time Mr. Olympia Dorian Yates and high-intensity-training pioneer Mike Mentzer. Little and his wife, Terri, are the owners of Nautilus North Strength & Fitness Centre (nautilusnorth.com), which *Ironman* magazine heralded as "one of the leading fitness research centers in North America." Little is a regular columnist for *Ironman* and the innovator of three revolutionary training protocols: Max Contraction Training, Static Contraction Training, and Power Factor Training. He is the author of more than thirty books ranging from bodybuilding and martial arts guides to scholarly tomes on history and philosophy. Little's methods have been called "revolutionary" by the bodybuilding community, and his articles on bodybuilding have been featured in every major health and fitness publication in North America, Europe, and Asia, while his training methods have been employed by more than 150,000 bodybuilders and strength athletes around the world.